fascinating facts:

fascinating facts:

by David Louis

 Ridge Press / Crown Publishers, Inc., New York

Editor-in-Chief: Jerry Mason
Editor: Adolph Suehsdorf
Art Director: Allan Mogel
Associate Editor: Ronne Peltzman
Associate Editor: Joan Fisher
Picture Editor: Marion Geisinger
Art Associate: Liney Li
Art Production: Doris Mullane

Prepared and produced by The Ridge Press.

Library of Congress Cataloging in Publication Data

Louis, David
  Fascinating facts.

    1. Curiosities and wonders. I. Title.
AG 243.C37 1977   001.9′3   77-7055
ISBN 0-517-53051-1
ISBN 0-517-53052-X pbk.

Printed in the United States of America.

Contents

Animals

The largest living species of kangaroo has a head the size of a sheep's and may stand 7 feet tall. An extinct species of kangaroo had a head the size of a Shetland pony's and reached a height of more than 10 feet. There are miniature kangaroos, such as the musk kangaroo, that are no bigger than a jackrabbit.

Greyhounds have the best eyesight of any breed of dog.

Every 9.6 years there is a peak in Canada's wildlife population, especially among muskrats, red fox, skunks, mink, lynx, and rabbits. The population of grasshoppers in the world tends to rise and fall rhythmically in 9.2-year cycles.

A rodent's teeth never stop growing. They are worn down by the animal's constant gnawing on bark, leaves, and other vegetable matter.

Beaver, one of the largest rodents in the world, gnawing on a tree branch

One million stray dogs and about 500,000 stray cats live in the New York City metropolitan area. There are about 100 million dogs and cats in the United States. Americans spend $5.4 billion on their pets each year. Every hour, 12,500 puppies are born in the United States.

Elephant herds post their own sentries. When danger threatens, the sentry raises its trunk and though it may be as far as a half-mile away, the rest of the herd is instantly alerted. How this communication takes place is not understood.

The whale has the slowest metabolism of all animals. Despite its great size, it lives on one of the smallest of all creatures, the microscopic plankton found throughout the sea.

A horse focuses its eye by changing the angle of its head, not by changing the shape of the lens of the eye, as humans do.

Deer have no gall bladders.

A mole can dig a tunnel 300 feet long in one night.

The average porcupine has more than 30,000 quills. Porcupines are excellent swimmers because their quills are hollow and serve as pontoons to keep them afloat.

Wildlife biologists estimate that as many as five out of six fawns starve to death during a hard winter in Vermont.

The now-extinct ancestor of the horse, eohippus, had a short neck, a pug muzzle, and stood no higher than a medium-sized dog.

The kinkajou's tail is twice as long as its body. Every night it wraps itself in its tail and uses it as a pillow.

The ring-tailed lemur, a primate found only on the island of Madagascar, meows like a cat.

Genuine ivory does not come only from elephants. It can come from the tusks of a boar or a walrus.

A horse can sleep standing up.

A rat can go without water longer than a camel can.

An elephant may consume 500 pounds of hay and 60 gallons of water in a single day.

Cats have no ability to taste sweet things.

There is no single cat called a panther. The name is commonly applied to the leopard, but it is also used to refer to the puma and the jaguar. A black panther is really a black leopard.

Guinea pigs were first domesticated by the Incas, who used them for food, in sacrifices, and as household pets.

A male baboon can kill a leopard.

The hippopotamus is born underwater.

Cows have four stomachs. Often when a calf is born the farmer will make it swallow a magnet. This is to attract the various nails, staples, tacks, bits of wire, and so on that the cow may ingest while grazing. (This odd hunger is known to farmers as "hardware disease.") When the animal is slaughtered, the butcher will remove the magnet along with the metallic debris and sell the mass of iron and steel for scrap.

The hippopotamus (*Hippopotamus amphibius*):

is, next to the elephant, the heaviest of all land mammals, larger even than the rhinoceros. It may weigh as much as 8,000 pounds.

is a close relative of the pig.

can open its mouth wide enough to accommodate a 4-foot-tall child.

has skin an inch and a half thick, so solid that most bullets cannot penetrate it.

has a stomach 10 feet long, capable of holding 6 bushels of grass.

The crocodile *(Crocodylus sp.):*

is a cannibal; it will occasionally eat other crocodiles.

does not chew its food, but swallows it whole. It carries several pounds of small stones in its stomach to aid in grinding up and digesting its nourishment.

does cry tears, but they are crocodile tears—not real tears at all, but glandular excretions that serve to expel excess salt from the eyes.

continually grows new sets of teeth to replace old teeth.

cannot move its tongue (a crocodile's tongue is rooted to the base of its mouth).

is surprisingly fast on land. If pursued by a crocodile, a person should run in a zigzag motion, for the crocodile has little or no ability to make sudden changes of direction.

The frigate bird can fly at a speed of 260 miles per hour. The snail moves at a rate of 0.000362005 miles per hour. The fastest animal on four legs is the cheetah, which races 70 miles per hour over short distances and can accelerate to 45 miles per hour in two seconds. An elephant, despite its ponderous appearance, can do 25 miles per hour on an open stretch, and a charging rhino has been clocked at 30. The fastest of all fish in the sea is the swordfish, streaming forward at 68 miles per hour. Man's best speed in the water is 4.1 miles per hour; the maximum speed at which a human being can run on land is 24 miles per hour.

A squirrel has no color vision; it sees only in black and white. Every part of its field of vision, however, is in perfect focus, not just straight ahead, as with man.

Weimaraner dogs were first bred in Germany for hunting deer in a special manner: the dogs were trained to pursue stags low and from behind, and to leap at their victims' genitals and rip off these most vulnerable organs in a single bite. Today, if given a chance, many members of this breed will instinctively perform the same feat.

A baby turkey is called a "poult." A group of lions is known as a "pride," and a group of hogs is a "herd." Geese in collection are a "gaggle," and when in the air they are a "skein." A gathering of foxes is referred to as a "skunkel," a gathering of quail as a "covey." A baby kangaroo is a "joey." A baby fish is a "fry."

An ox is a castrated bull. A mule is a sterile cross between a male ass and a female horse. A donkey is an ass, but an ass is not always a donkey. The word "ass" refers to any of several hoofed mammals of the genus *Equus,* including the onager.

A kangaroo cannot jump if its tail is lifted off the ground. It needs its tail for pushing off.

Snakes picking up sound vibrations by flicking their tongues

A snake has no ears. However, its tongue is extremely sensitive to sound vibrations, and by constantly flicking its tongue the snake picks up these sound waves. In this sense a snake "hears" with its tongue.

Contrary to popular belief, dogs do not sweat by salivating. They sweat through the pads of their feet.

When a hippopotamus exerts itself, gets angry, or stays out of the water for too long, it exudes red sweatlike mucus through its skin.

Every day of the year 100 whales are killed by whale fish-ermen.

Early U.S. whaling ship off California coast

A newborn Chinese water deer is so small it can almost be held in the palm of the hand.

Every year more people are killed in Africa by crocodiles than by lions.

Antlers and horns are not the same. Horns grow throughout an animal's life and are found on both the male and female of a species (such as a cow). Antlers, composed of a differ-ent chemical substance, are shed every year. Usually, though not invariably, they are found on males.

A hippopotamus can run faster than a man.

The Mojave ground squirrel, found mainly in the American West, hibernates for two-thirds of every year.

The sea lion (Eumetopias jubata):
    can swim 6,000 miles, stopping only to sleep.
    is susceptible to sunburn, and if put on board a ship will get as seasick as man.
    Male sea lions may have more than 100 wives and sometimes go three months without eating.
    There once were more sea lions on earth than people.

The venom of the king cobra is so deadly that one gram of it can kill 150 people. Just to handle the substance can put one in a coma.

A whale's heart beats only nine times a minute.

A cat uses its whiskers to determine if a space is too small to squeeze through. The whiskers act as feelers or antennae, helping the animal to judge the precise width of any narrow passage.

King cobra

Of all known forms of animal life ever to inhabit the earth, only about 10 percent still exist today.

The lesser mole rat not only digs an entire subterranean house for itself, complete with storerooms, halls, bedrooms, and a "wedding chamber" where all mating takes place, but actually constructs a separate bathroom which, when used, is sealed off from the rest of the house.

Elephants are covered with hair. Although it is not apparent from a distance, at close range one can discern a thin coat of light hairs covering practically every part of an elephant's body.

Male monkeys lose the hair on their heads in the same way men do.

The flying snake of Java and Malaysia *(Chrysopelea ornata)* is able to flatten itself out like a ribbon and sail like a glider from tree to tree.

A good milking cow will give nearly 6,000 quarts of milk every year.

There are buffalo in Poland. They live mainly in the area of the Bialowieza Forest and are known as *zubra*. The well-known Polish vodka Zubrowka, which means "buffalo brand," takes its name from these animals.

Sheep will not drink from running water. Hence the line in the Twenty-third Psalm: "He leadeth me beside the still waters."

A completely blind chameleon will still take on the colors of its environment.

Camels were used as pack animals in Nevada and Arizona as late as 1870.

Male moose have antlers 7 feet across. The antlers often weigh 60 pounds.

The fur of the vicuña, a small member of the camel family which lives only in the Andes Mountains of Peru, is so fine that each hair is less than two-thousandths of an inch thick. The animal was considered sacred by the Incas, and only royalty could wear its fleece.

A female mouse may spawn as many as ten litters of eight to ten young during her lifetime—which generally is less than a year. The gestation period is three weeks, and the young mice reach maturity in only ten weeks.

The chameleon, a small lizard generally measuring 6 or 7 inches, has a tongue several inches longer than its body. With a thrust of this remarkable appendage it can catch insects some 10 inches away.

The bat is the only mammal that can fly.

A pig is a hog—hog is a generic name for all swine—but a hog is not a pig. In the terminology of hog raising, a pig is a baby hog less than ten weeks old.

The bottle-nosed whale can dive to a depth of 3,000 feet in two minutes.

Architecture & Construction

The Egyptian pyramids were once faced completely with marble. The Parthenon was once painted.

Nobody knows who built the Taj Mahal. The names of the architects, masons, and designers that have come down to us have all proved to be latter-day inventions, and there is no evidence to indicate who the real creators were.

Boulder Dam is as thick at its base (660 feet) as a city block is long.

The Washington Monument sinks 6 inches every year.

The Statue of Liberty's mouth is 3 feet wide.

The largest pyramid in the world is not in Egypt but in Cholulu de Rivadahia, Mexico. It is 177 feet tall and covers 25 acres. It was built sometime between 6 and 12 A.D.

Bricks are the oldest manufactured building material still in use. Egyptians used them 7,000 years ago.

The world's two largest dams are both in Russia. They are the Inguri (988 feet high) and the Nurek (984 feet high).

Face of Statue of
Liberty before assemblage

There is a house in Rockport, Massachusetts, built entirely of newspaper. The Paper House at Pigeon Cove, as it is called, is made of 215 thicknesses of newspaper. "All the furniture is made of newspaper," its builder reports, "including a desk of newspapers relating Lindbergh's historic flight."

The pyramids in Egypt contain enough stone and mortar to construct a wall 10 feet high and 5 feet wide running from New York City to Los Angeles.

Empire State Building

Many of the first houses in the American colonies (including the home of William Penn) were built from bricks used as ballast in the holds of ships. These ships arrived in the New World filled with bricks, the bricks were unloaded and sold, and the cargo hatches were refilled with export goods in their place. The bricks were then used by the colonists to construct their homes.

In 1830 the Taj Mahal was sold to a British merchant who planned to dismantle it stone by stone and ship the marble back to England, where it would be used to embellish English estates. Though wrecking machinery was brought into the gardens of the Taj, the plan was discouraged: the project turned out to be too expensive.

In 1931 an industrialist named Robert Ilg built a half-size replica of the Leaning Tower of Pisa outside Chicago and lived in it for several years. The tower is still there.

In the city of Washington, D.C., no building may be built taller than the Capitol.

The Empire State Building (1,250 feet) exceeds the height of the Eiffel Tower (984.5 feet) by only 265.5 feet.

The Empire State Building was built with 60,000 tons of steel, 3 million square feet of wire mesh, 70,000 cubic yards of concrete, 10 million bricks, and can accommodate 15,000 people.

In 1711, when work on St. Paul's Cathedral in London was completed and was shown to George I, the King is reported to have exclaimed to its architect, Christopher Wren, that the work was "aweful" and "artificial." In the eighteenth century, "aweful" meant awe-inspiring, and "artificial" meant full of great art.

Art & Artists

During the Napoleonic Wars, Napoleon's soldiers bivouacked in the chapel of Santa Maria delle Grazie in Milan, where Leonardo's *Last Supper* is located. The soldiers used the painting in target practice, shooting at the central figure of Christ's head. This is why the face of Christ is almost obliterated in the painting.

The largest stained-glass window in the world is at Kennedy International Airport in New York City. It can be seen on the American Airlines terminal building and measures 300 feet long by 23 feet high.

Indian-miniature painters of the Kangra school used brushes so fine that they were sometimes made of a single hair. A painter of Indian miniatures would often apprentice for ten years before he was allowed to pick up a brush. The colors used by this school of artists were made of such strange substances as crushed beetles, ground lapis lazuli, and blood.

The statue by Auguste Rodin that has come to be called *The Thinker* was not meant to be a portrait of man in thought. It is a portrait of the poet Dante.

There is only one picture by an American hanging in the Louvre—*Whistler's Mother*. *Whistler's Mother*, however, is only the painting's popular name; its official title is *Arrangement in Black and Gray: The Artist's Mother*.

In his last days, the painter Pierre Renoir was so crippled

with arthritis that he had to have the brushes tied to his arms in order to execute his paintings.

Equestrian statues: traditionally when all four of the horse's hooves are on the ground, it signifies that the rider died a natural death. One hoof in the air indicates that he died of wounds sustained in action. If two are raised, it means that the rider was killed on the field of battle.

Peter Paul Rubens

The seventeenth-century Flemish artist Peter Paul Rubens often did not paint his own pictures. His procedure was to set up the canvas, draw in preliminary outlines, sketch in the various figures, and design the color scheme. He turned the actual painting over to members of his atelier, a veritable factory of skilled painters, some of whom specialized in painting flowers, some in fruit, some in birds, candles, or even beards. Van Dyck, one of the greatest of all Flemish painters, was a member of this great studio.

The horns protruding from the head of the famous statue of Moses by Michelangelo were a mistake! It is true that the Bible describes Moses as having horns coming from his head. This, however, was an error on the part of the translators. In Hebrew the words for "horn" and "ray of light" are spelled identically. The translators misinterpreted "ray" for "horn" and thus Moses is often portrayed in western art as looking like a devil.

Detail of Michelangelo's
Moses

The Spanish painter Velázquez was official court painter to King Philip IV when he was twenty-six.

Currier and Ives published more than 7,000 prints. They ran a large factory with hundreds of employees, including many full-staff artists. Though their prints are rare and expensive today, they originally sold for 10 cents apiece.

Things you may not know about the *Mona Lisa:*

She has no eyebrows (it was the fashion in Renaissance Florence to shave them off).

The real name of the painting is not *Mona Lisa.* It is *La Giaconda.* It is a portrait of a middle-class Florentine woman, the wife of a merchant named Francesco del Giacondo.

The painting measures less than 2 feet by 2 feet.

An entire opera was written about the painting by Max von Schillings.

X-rays of the *Mona Lisa* show that there are three completely different versions of the same subject, all painted by Leonardo, under the final portrait.

Ancient Chinese artists freely painted scenes of nakedness and coition. Never, absolutely never, would they depict a simple bare female foot.

Detail of 12th-century Chinese painting of women preparing silk. Note that girl's and woman's feet are not shown.

Aviation

Houdini was the first man to fly an airplane solo in Australia.

The top of the tower on the Empire State Building was originally intended (though never used) as a mooring place for dirigibles.

According to the Federal Aviation Authority, United States airlines are four times safer than the airlines of any other country.

The name of the first airplane flown at Kitty Hawk by the Wright Brothers was *Bird of Prey.* The maiden flight of the

Bird of Prey, however, was less than a flight—the plane stayed in the air only long enough to sail 59 feet.

Charles Lindbergh was not the first man to fly the Atlantic. He was the sixty-seventh. The first sixty-six made the crossing in dirigibles and twin-engine mail planes. Lindbergh was the first to make the dangerous flight *alone.*

Castor oil is used as a lubricant in jet planes.

An airplane uses more fuel flying at 25,000 feet than at 30,000 feet. The higher it flies, the thinner the atmosphere and the less atmospheric resistance it must buck.

Babies & Birth

Newborn babies are not blind. Studies have shown that newborns have approximately 20/50 vision and can easily discriminate between degrees of brightness.

A fetus in the womb can hear. Tests have shown that fetuses respond to various sounds just as vigorously as they respond to pressures and internal sensations.

A survey conducted at Iowa State College in 1969 suggests that a parent's stress at the time of conception plays a major role in determining a baby's sex. The child tends to be of the same sex as the parent who is under less stress.

Statistics based on more than a half-million births occurring in New York City hospitals between 1948 and 1957 show a significantly greater number of births taking place during the waning moon than during the waxing moon.

Until the 1920's, babies in Finland were delivered in saunas. The heat was thought to help combat infection, and the warm atmosphere was considered pleasing to the infant.

Children born in the month of May are on the average 200 grams heavier at birth than children born in any other month.

Up to the age of six or seven months a child can breathe and swallow at the same time. An adult cannot do this. (Try it.)

Midgets and dwarfs almost always have normal-sized children, even if both parents are midgets or dwarfs.

Twins are born less frequently in the eastern part of the world than in the western.

The Bible

Studies of the Dead Sea Scrolls indicate that the passage in the Bible known as the Sermon on the Mount is actually an ancient Essene prayer dating to hundreds of years before the birth of Christ.

The American Bible Association has published almost a billion Bibles since it was founded in 1816.

The Lord's Prayer appears twice in the Bible, in Matthew VI and Luke XI.

Two chapters in the Bible, 2 Kings 19 and Isaiah 37, are alike almost word for word.

The shortest verse in the Bible consists of two words: "Jesus wept" (John 11:35).

The King James version of the Bible has 50 authors, 66 books, 1,189 chapters, and 31,173 verses.

In the history of printing, several early English Bibles are famous not so much for their workmanship or their beauty as for their textual idiosyncrasies. A few famous examples, much sought after by rare-Bible collectors, are:

The Breeches Bible (1560)—so named because it states that Adam and Eve "sewed fig tree leaves together and made themselves breeches."

The Bug Bible (1551)—so named because of an incorrect translation of a line in the Ninety-first Psalm. The line "Thou shalt not be afraid for the terror by night" reads "Thou shalt not be afraid of any buggies by night."

The Treacle Bible (1568)—so named because it uses the word "treacle" for "balm" in the line "Is there no balm in Gilead?"

Birds

Eagle with young deer in its talons

An eagle can attack, kill, and carry away an animal as large as a young deer. The harpy eagle of South America feeds on monkeys.

The penculine titmouse of Africa builds its home in such a sturdy manner that Masai tribesmen use their nests for purses and carrying cases.

The female knot-tying weaverbird will refuse to mate with a male who has built a shoddy nest. If spurned, the male must take the nest apart and completely rebuild it in order to win the affections of the female.

The average hummingbird weighs less than a penny. It has a body temperature of 111 degrees and beats its wings more than 75 times a second. Its newborn are the size of bumblebees and its nest is the size of a walnut. The hummingbird is the only bird that can fly backward.

When attacked, the petrel, a giant bird of the Antarctic, repels its enemies either by regurgitating food in their faces or by squirting a jet of viscous oil from its nostrils with a force great enough to knock down a person.

Bald eagles are not bald. The top of their head is covered with slicked-down white feathers; from a distance they appear hairless.

The tailorbird of Africa makes its nest by sewing together two broad leaves. It uses fiber as the thread and its bill as the needle.

In one year, hens in America lay enough eggs to encircle the globe a hundred times.

Male bowerbirds build and decorate nests to be used exclusively for mating. They ornament the nests with flowers, bits of string, berries, feathers, even pieces of glass or brightly colored paper. After these decorations are in place, the male bowerbird paints the entire nest with blueberry juice that he has extracted by pressing the berries in his beak. After courtship and mating have taken place, the nest is deserted and a separate one is constructed for rearing the young.

Flamingos are not naturally pink. They get their color from their food, tiny blue-green algae that turn pink during digestion.

In 1880 there were approximately 2 billion passenger pigeons in the United States. By 1914 the species was extinct.

Above: Flamingos
Left: Passenger pigeon

The penguin has an apparatus above its eyes that enables it to transform salt water into fresh. The penguin takes only one mate during its life and is such a conscientious parent that it will, if necessary, starve to death in order to provide its children with food.

The albatross drinks sea water. It has a special desalinization apparatus that strains out and excretes all excess salt.

The optimum depth of birdbath water, says the Audubon Society of America, is 2½ inches. Less water makes it difficult for birds to take a bath; more makes them afraid.

Ducks will lay eggs only in the early morning.

An ostrich egg can make eleven and a half omelets.

The Body

A sneeze can travel as fast as 100 miles per hour.

Above: 19th-century "hearing aid" Below: Nose and nasal cavity

As men and women get older their ability to hear high-pitched sounds diminishes. The ability to taste sweet foods also decreases with age.

The human nose can detect the odor of artificial musk in such low concentrations as one part musk to 32 billion parts of air.

The easiest sounds for the human ear to hear, and those which carry best when pronounced, are, in order, "ah," "aw," "eh," "ee," and "oo."

The sound heard by a listener when holding a seashell to his ear does *not* come from the shell itself. It is the echo of the blood pulsing in the listener's own ear.

A person's nose and ears continue to grow throughout his or her life.

The nose cleans, warms, and humidifies over 500 cubic feet of air every day.

Human eyes are so sensitive that on a clear night when there is no moon, a person sitting on a mountain peak can see a match struck 50 miles away.

It is impossible to sneeze and keep one's eyes open at the same time.

While reading a page of print the eyes do not move continually across the page. They move in a series of jumps, called "fixations," from one clump of words to the next.

Two out of three adults in the United States wear glasses at some time.

It takes the human eyes an hour to adapt completely to seeing in the dark. Once adapted, however, the eyes are about 100,000 times more sensitive to light than they are in bright sunlight.

The human eyes can perceive more than 1 million simultaneous visual impressions and are able to discriminate among nearly 8 million gradations of color.

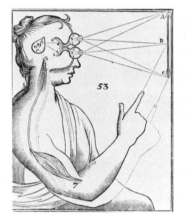

The average person's field of vision is 180 degrees.

Sight accounts for 90 to 95 percent of all sensory perceptions.

The pupil of the eye expands as much as 45 percent when a person looks at something pleasing.

Blue eyes are the most sensitive to light, dark brown the least sensitive.

17th-century woodcut showing how image of arrow is transmitted from eyes to brain

It takes 17 muscles to smile, 43 muscles to frown.

The average person's hand flexes its finger joints 25 million times during a lifetime.

One-fourth of the 206 bones in the human body are located in the feet.

Drinking *lowers* rather than raises the body temperature. There is an illusion of heat because alcohol causes the capillaries to dilate and fill with blood. In very cold weather drinking alcoholic beverages can lead to frostbite.

The strongest bone in the body, the thigh bone, is hollow. Ounce for ounce it has a greater pressure tolerance and bearing strength than a rod of equivalent size cast in solid steel.

Type O is the most common blood type in the world. Type AB is the rarest. There is also a subtype called A-H, but to date only three people in the world are known to have it.

The substance that human blood resembles most closely in terms of chemical composition is sea water.

There are almost 6 million red blood cells in a cubic millimeter of human blood. The entire body contains about 30 trillion red blood cells. When a person inhales several breaths of carbon monoxide, more than half of the blood's hemoglobin combines with the gas, leaving only half the red blood cells to carry oxygen. This has the same effect on the body as a sudden loss of 50 percent of one's red blood cells. Fifteen million red blood cells are produced and an equal number are destroyed every second.

The average brain comprises 2 percent of a person's total body weight. Yet it requires 25 percent of all oxygen used by the body, as opposed to 12 percent used by the kidneys and 7 percent by the heart.

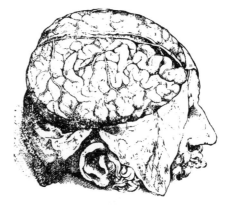

The body has 70,000 miles of blood vessels. The heart pumps blood through this labyrinth and back again once every minute.

A person breathes 7 quarts of air every minute.

The average person takes from twelve to eighteen breaths per minute.

The right lung takes in more air than the left.

The human brain is 80 percent water, more watery than our blood.

The human brain is insensitive to pain. The suffering of a headache comes not from the organ itself but from the nerves and muscles lining it.

Neanderthal man, the first human being in the true sense, had a brain capacity 100 cc larger than modern man's.

The average human heart beats about 100,000 times every 24 hours. In a seventy-two-year lifetime the heart beats more than 2.5 billion times.

A woman's heart beats faster than a man's.

During pregnancy, the uterus expands to 500 times its normal size.

During menstruation, the sensitivity of a woman's middle finger is reduced.

The human tongue tastes bitter things with the taste buds toward the back. Salty and pungent flavors are tasted in the middle of the tongue, sweet flavors at the tip.

The average person's total skin covering would weigh about 6 pounds if collected into one mass.

The average woman's thighs are 1½ inches larger in circumference than the average man's.

An average man on an average day excretes 2½ quarts of sweat.

The palms of the hands and soles of the feet contain more sweat glands than any other part of the body.

A skin graft can be taken only from the skin of one's own body or from the body of an identical twin.

False teeth are often radioactive. Approximately 1 million Americans wear some form of denture; half of these dentures are made of a porcelain compound laced with minute amounts of uranium to stimulate fluorescence. Without the uranium additive the dentures would be a dull green color when seen under artificial light.

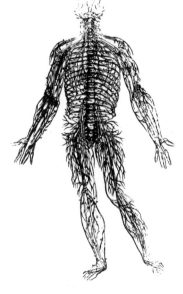

16th-century drawing by Andreas Vesalius showing network of nerves in human body

For many years after the Battle of Waterloo, dentures known as "Waterloo teeth" were sold throughout Europe. These were actual human teeth extracted from the corpses of soldiers on the Waterloo battlefield. They were especially esteemed among denture wearers because most of them came from young, healthy boys.

The older a person gets the less sleep he requires. A child should get from 8 to 9 hours a night. An elderly adult can do well with 4 to 6 hours.

The liver is a gland, not an organ.

There are 10 trillion living cells in the human body.

Tongue prints are as unique as fingerprints.

The human body has 45 miles of nerves.

The fingernails and the hair are dead. Both are made of a tissue called keratin, which is similar to the dried skin cells that continually flake off the body. Hair and nails, however, originate from living cells. Growth occurs at the base, and new cells push the dead hair and nails upward. Then these cells themselves die, to be pushed up and replaced by more from below.

While 7 men in 100 have some form of color blindness, only 1 woman in 1,000 suffers from it. The most common form of color blindness is a red-green deficiency.

The mouth produces a quart of saliva a day.

Human nails and hair do *not* grow after death. They are simply the last part of the body to disintegrate.

The fingernails grow faster on the hand you favor. If you are right-handed your right fingernails will grow faster; if left-handed, your left. The middle fingernail grows faster than all other nails.

China

In *Tales from Early Histories,* the Chinese historian Ssu-ma relates that the Yin dynasty king, Chou-hsin (1154–1122 B.C.) used the following mixtures as aphrodisiacs:

The Hunting Lion—the paws of bears simmered over a slow fire, and flavored with the horn of a rhinoceros and distilled human urine.

Celestial Thunder—the tongues of a hundred peacocks spiced with chili powder from the western provinces and flavored with the sperm of pubescent boys.

Three-Day Glory—soy beans mixed with fresh ginseng, the penis of an ox, and dried human placenta.

In ancient China, towns were often arranged in specific patterns so that if seen from the air the whole community resembled an animal or a symbolic design. The city of Tsuenchen-fu was built in the shape of a carp. Wung-chun was laid out in the shape of a fish net. Other towns were arranged to resemble snakes, stars, sunbursts, and dragons.

In sixteenth- and seventeenth-century Peking, one took revenge against one's enemies by placing finely chopped tiger's whiskers in their food. The numerous infinitesimal whisker barbs would get caught in the vicitim's digestive tract and cause hundreds of painful sores and infections.

The famous Boxer Rebellion in China received its name from its association with an ancient Chinese martial art, Kung-fu. During this bloody uprising in northern China in 1900, traditionalist members of a secret society called *I-ho-ch'uan* ("Harmonious and Righteous Fists") set out to destroy all foreign influences in China, including schools, churches, and places of commerce and trade. The members of this society were well trained in the ancient fighting art of Kung-fu, which, because there was no equivalent word in English to describe it, became known to westerners simply as "boxing." Hence the uprising was termed the "Boxers' Rebellion."

In third-century China, kites were used as games, ritual objects, musical instruments, transmitters of messages, distance-measuring devices, weapons, and parachutes.

The willow-leaf pattern commonly found on Chinese plates and cookware is descended from a series of signs and emblems used by ancient Chinese secret societies. The original pattern, designed in the fifteenth century and used as a means of communication among members of these societies, was discovered by the Manchu government, which ordered all the plates destroyed. The pattern turned up again in Europe in the eighteenth century. It had been copied by a western merchant who had managed to smuggle a few of the original plates out of China.

In the early fifteenth century, scholars in China compiled an encyclopedia consisting of 11,095 volumes.

The men who served as guards along the Great Wall of China in the Middle Ages were often born on the wall, grew up there, married there, died there, and were buried within it. Many of these guards never left the wall in their entire lives.

Chang Hsien-chung, a Chinese bandit, is credited with having killed 40 million people between 1643 and 1648. He completely wiped out the population of Szechwan province.

At funerals in ancient China, when the lid of a coffin was closed, mourners took a few steps backward lest their shadows get caught in the box.

In ancient China people committed suicide by eating a pound of salt.

There are more than 40,000 characters in Chinese script.

Some Chinese typewriters have 5,700 characters. The keyboard is almost 3 feet wide on some models, and the fastest one can type on these machines is 11 words per minute.

Until the modernization of China, and to some extent still today, the Chinese did the following things:

When they met a friend they shook their own hand, not his.

When serving tea they placed the saucer over the cup (to keep it warm), not under it.

They drank hot beverages to cool themselves.

After bathing they dried themselves with a wet towel.

When building a house they constructed the roof first.

Their compasses pointed south, not north.

They said "westsouth," not "southwest."

Their surnames came first, not last.

They addressed letters in the following manner: New York City, Street Blank, 50, Jones, John Mr.

They read books from back to front and put footnotes at the top of the page.

Noon was any time between 12:00 and 2:00 P.M., midnight any hour before dawn.

They used paper in their windows instead of glass.

Centuries before Christ, the Chinese were using natural gas for lighting. Gas was brought to the surface from beds of rock salt 1,600 feet beneath the ground, conveyed through bamboo pipes, and used for illuminating home interiors in Szechwan province.

Confucius is not a Chinese name. In China the sage's name is K'ung Fu-tzu. Further, the words "mandarin," "junk," "coolie," and "pagoda" are all English. None of them is Chinese in origin.

In the Chinese written language, the ideograph that stands for "trouble" represents two women under one roof.

The abacus was not invented in China. It originated in Egypt in 2000 B.C., almost a millennium before it reached the Orient.

The Chinese invented eyeglasses. Marco Polo reported seeing many pairs worn by the Chinese as early as 1275, 500 years before lens grinding became an art in the West.

Confucius, from a design of the Tang dynasty (7th–10th century)

Churches

The first gold brought back by Christopher Columbus from the Americas was used to gild the ceiling of the church of Santa Maria Maggiore in Rome. The ceiling and the gold are still there.

In the original architectural design, the French cathedral of Chartres had six spires. (It was built with two spires.)

Many Gothic churches of the Middle Ages were built in the following way: a quarry site was established, often as much as 50 miles from the place where the church was to be erected. When the rocks were mined, volunteers from all over the countryside would form a living chain from the quarry to the building site. The rocks would then be passed from hand to hand all the way to the construction grounds.

The world's largest Gothic cathedral is in New York City. It is the Cathedral of St. John the Divine on Amsterdam Ave-

nue and 112th Street. The cathedral measures 601 feet long, 146 feet wide, and has a transept measuring 320 feet from end to end.

The Classical World

Nero did not fiddle while Rome burned. The fiddle had not yet been invented. Nor was Nero there. He was at his villa in Antium, 50 miles away.

The Colosseum of ancient Rome was occasionally filled with water and an entire naval battle was staged there, complete with armed vessels and fights to the death.

Remains of the Roman Colosseum

The ancient Greeks were the first to use bed springs. They fashioned them out of braided leather thongs and hung them between opposite sides of the bed.

At the time of Titus in fourth-century Rome, the Circus Maximus held 380,000 spectators.

According to several Greek historians, the great playwright Aeschylus was killed by a tortoise dropped on his head from a great height by an eagle.

Florentine engraving depicting the death of Aeschylus

The Roman pantheon included a god whose only function was to rule over mildew. His name was Robigus. Each year on April 25th a procession wound through the streets of Rome to Robigus' sacred grove, where a red puppy was sacrificed in his name. The Romans hoped the sacrifice would appease the mildew god's hunger for their crops.

Until the time of the Caesars, all Romans were vegetarians.

Suetonius Tranquillis reported in his *Life of Augustus* that the great Roman poet Vergil once held a funeral for a dead fly, complete with pallbearers and lengthy eulogies. In ancient Rome, cemetery land was not taxable. By interring a fly on the land surrounding his private villa, the wily poet turned his home into a burial ground and thus made it tax-exempt.

Ancient Romans always entered the home of a friend on their right foot—the left side of the body was thought to portend evil. The Latin word for "left" is *sinister*—thus our English word "sinister" for anything threatening or malevolent.

Christmas-tree ornaments date back to the time of the Romans. During the Saturnalia, which coincided roughly with our Christmas holiday, the Romans hung little masks of Bacchus on pine trees. Vergil refers to these dangling ornaments as *oscilla,* and describes how during the December season evergreens were laden with them.

Roman coins minted during the reign of Diocletian have been excavated in remote parts of Iceland. No one is quite certain what this signifies historically, as the very existence of Iceland was unknown to the ancient Romans.

The ancient Greek leader Pericles was so self-conscious about his pointed head that he would only pose for portraits wearing a helmet.

Roman statues were made with detachable heads, so that one head could be removed and replaced by another.

The month of July is named after Julius Caesar. The month of August is named after Augustus Caesar.

The Roman emperor Caligula bestowed the rank of Consul First Class on his favorite horse, Incitatus. The horse was provided with a gold goblet for drinking wine and with an ivory manger.

Atomic theory was known to the ancient Greeks. It formed the basis of the Greek philosopher Democritus' theory of "atomism" and his "materialistic" explanation of the universe.

In ancient Greece, no one was born or died on the island of Delos. Whenever someone became pregnant or ill, she or he was quickly removed from the sacred island and was kept away until nature took its course.

In ancient Rome it was considered a sign of leadership to be born with a hooked nose.

A stone phallus was set above the city gates of many ancient Roman towns as a protection against bad luck. Under the phallus appeared the inscription *Hic Habit Felicitas*— "Happiness Dwells Here." The Romans often hung small phalli around children's necks as a protection against the evil eye.

Above: Pericles
Below: Roman statuette of theatrical figure with hooked nose

The level and the claw hammer, found in every modern carpenter's tool chest, were invented by the ancient Romans.

Colleges

The University of Calcutta has 175,000 students.

According to a survey taken by the Standard & Poor Corporation in 1976, 30 percent of the leading executives of United States corporations attended the following twelve colleges: Harvard leads the list and is followed, in order, by New York University, Yale, University of Pennsylvania, University of Michigan, Columbia, Northwestern, City College of New York, Princeton, University of Wisconsin, MIT, and University of Illinois.

John Harvard did not found Harvard University. Harvard, a Puritan minister, simply left his library of 400 books to the college when he died in 1638. The college itself had been founded two years earlier and was first known as Cambridge.

Yale was founded by Harvard men. In 1700 ten educators, nine of them Harvard graduates, met in Killingworth (now Clinton), Connecticut, for the purpose of establishing a college. When it was begun, Yale was not known as Yale but as the Collegiate School of Connecticut. Only in 1718, thanks to donations from Elihu Yale, was it given its present name.

Yale College and
State House, New Haven,
early 19th century

The famous goldfish-swallowing fad was started at Harvard University in 1938 by a student who downed a fish on a lark, then was challenged to perform the same feat in public. Hundreds of students witnessed the performance, and the fad caught on. The first goldfish-swallowing record was set the following year by a student from Middlesex College who downed 67 live goldfish. In 1967 the fad was revived just long enough for a St. Joseph's College undergrad to consume 199 hapless fish.

There are fewer than a million college graduates each year in the United States.

North Texas State University gives a degree in "dance-band arts."

Dartmouth was the only college in New England to remain open during the entire Revolutionary War.

When Harvard College was founded in 1636 it was surrounded by a tall stockade to keep out prowling wolves and hostile Indians.

Comic Strips & Cartoons

Mickey Mouse has only four fingers. Early Mickey Mouses can be distinguished from later ones by the fact that the originals have a pie-shaped section of white in their eyes while the later ones do not.

The oldest continuous comic strip still in existence is "The Katzenjammer Kids." It first appeared in newspapers in 1897.

There is a 6-foot-high stone monument dedicated to the comic-strip character Popeye in Crystal City, Texas.

Communications

The *Boston Nation,* a newspaper published in Ohio during the mid-nineteenth century, had pages 7½ feet long and 5½ feet wide. It required two people to hold the paper in proper reading position.

Almost half the newspapers in the world are published in the United States and Canada.

Of all professionals in the United States, journalists are credited with having the largest vocabulary—approximately 20,000 words. Clergymen, lawyers, and doctors each have about 15,000 words at their disposal. Skilled workers who have not had a college education know between 5,000 and 7,000 words, farm laborers about 1,600.

As of 1976, there were 110,200,000 TV sets in America, 372,000,000 radios, and 125,142,000 telephones.

The average American's vocabulary contains 10,000 words.

There is no known way for a submarine to communicate with land via radio when it is underwater.

According to a Nielsen rating survey taken in 1974, the average three-year-old child in America spends 30 hours a week in front of the television set.

There are more television sets in the United States than there are people in Japan.

As of 1976 in Greece, it cost $250 to get a telephone installed in a private residence and there was a four-year waiting list. The cost per call, however, is cheaper in Greece than in any other country in the world.

When using the first pay telephones (installed in an office building in New Haven, Connecticut, in June, 1880), a caller did not deposit his coins in the machine. He gave them to an attendant who stood next to the telephone. Coin telephones did not appear until 1899.

The first operators employed by the Bell Telephone Company were young boys who worked standing up. Only after several years did it occur to anybody to provide them with chairs.

The Pentagon building in Arlington, Virginia, has 68,000 miles of telephone lines.

There are 5,919,682 telephones in New York City, more phones than in the entire country of Spain. The cables serving the New York City area have 33,072,975 miles of wire.

On November 9, 1965, the day of the great blackout in the northeastern United States, 62 million phone calls were placed in New York City during a twenty-four-hour period. That is the greatest number of telephone calls ever made in one day.

There is only one country in the world without telephone service: Bhutan.

The average American sees or hears 560 advertisements a day.

Crime

The nation with the highest murder rate in the world is Nicaragua—there are 30 homicides per 100,000 people every year. As of 1975, the western nation with the lowest murder rate was Spain, with one killing per million people per year. In Hunza, a small state above Kashmir, only one murder has been recorded in the last seventy-five years.

Marie-Augustin Marquis de Pélier of Brittany was arrested in 1786 and spent the next fifty years of his life in prison. His crime: whistling at Queen Marie Antoinette as she was being ushered into a theater.

A 1975 Gallup poll shows that Latin America has the highest crime rate in the world. Next come Africa and then the United States. According to this poll, people from richer countries report themselves happier, find their lives more interesting, worry less, and would like fewer changes in their existence than those from more impoverished nations. Only 8 percent of Latin Americans and 6 percent of Africans are satisfied with their lives.

According to the National Safety Council, an average of sixty-nine people a day are shot to death with handguns in the United States. Three-quarters of these shootings take place within the inner family circle or among close friends.

According to the International Association of Art Security, art theft is the second most common international crime in the world (the first is narcotics smuggling). In 1975 33,840 thefts were reported world-wide. The United States had the greatest number of art robberies—9,460.

Approximately half the money paid out by fire-insurance companies in the United States is paid for fire loss due to arson.

Murder is the only crime that does not increase during the full moon. Theft, disorderly conduct, larceny, armed robbery, assault and battery, illegal breaking and entering, and rape all statistically increase dramatically during the full moon.

The Center for Studies in Criminology and Criminal Law at the University of Pennsylvania reports that as of 1975 women were responsible for 31 percent of all embezzlement in the United States.

Approximately 80 percent of the men serving terms in American prisons for rape were convicted not of forcible rape but of statutory rape, that is, of fornicating with a girl who is underage.

Death

After his death, Alexander the Great's remains were preserved in a huge crock of honey. Among the ancient Egyptians, it was common practice to bury the dead in this manner.

Undertakers report that human bodies do not deteriorate as quickly as they used to. The reason for this, they believe, is that the modern diet contains so many preservatives that these chemicals tend to prevent the body from decomposing too rapidly after death.

Obsidian balls, or occasionally brass balls, were placed in

Mummy from the tomb of Tutankhamen, 18th century B.C.

the eye sockets of Egyptian mummies. The bandaging of a mummy often took from six to eight months and required a collection of special tools, including a long metal hook that was used to draw the dead person's brains out through his nose.

When a man died in ancient Egypt, the females in his family would smear their heads and faces with mud and wander through the city beating themselves and tearing off their clothes.

When a crusader died, his corpse was chopped up and the flesh boiled away. This was done so that the skeleton could be conveniently returned to Europe for a Christian burial.

When a person dies, hearing is generally the last sense to go. The first sense lost is usually sight. Then follow taste, smell, and touch.

In ancient Egypt, when merchants left the country on business trips they carried small stone models of themselves. If they died while abroad, these figures were sent back to Egypt for proxy burial.

In Turkey the color of mourning is violet. In most Moslem countries and in China the color is white.

Among the Danakil tribesmen of Ethiopia, when a male dies his grave is marked with a stone for every man he killed.

Until the 1950's, Tibetans disposed of their dead by taking the body up to a hill, hacking it into little pieces, and feeding the remains to the birds.

It is possible to drown and not die. Technically the term "drowning" refers to the process of taking water into the lungs, not to death caused by that process.

More men than women commit suicide in the United States.

A recent Gallup poll shows that 69 percent of Americans

believe they will go somewhere after death.

Demography

In the tenth century A.D. there was not one city in Europe with a population over 400,000.

The black population of Houston, Texas (316,551), is greater than the total population of the entire state of Alaska (302,173).

No one knows how many people live in the country of Bhutan. As of 1975, no census had ever been taken.

In 1790 only 5 percent of the American population lived in cities.

The population of Colombia doubles every twenty-two years.

The population of the American colonies in 1610 was 350.

As of 1976, Chile, Egypt, and Guatemala had the highest birth rates in the world.

Ninety million people are added to the world's population each year. It is estimated that by the year 2000 there will be 1,800,000,000 people in China alone.

Hawaii is the only state in the United States where male life expectancy exceeds 70 years. Hawaii also leads all states in life expectancy in general, with an average of 73.6 years for both males and females.

Every year one out of five American families changes its place of residence.

Roughly a quarter of the world's people live in China.

There are more people in New York City (7,895,563) than

there are in the states of Alaska (302,173), Vermont (444,732), Wyoming (332,416), South Dakota (666,257), New Hampshire (737,681), Nevada (488,738), Idaho (713,008), Utah (1,059,273), Hawaii (769,913), North Dakota (617,761), Delaware (548,104), and New Mexico (1,016,000) combined.

If the population of the world continues to expand at its present rate, in the year 2100 there will be 60,000,000,-000,000,000 people on the face of the earth.

Roughly 40 percent of the population of the underdeveloped world is under fifteen years old.

The population of the entire world in 5000 B.C., according to the National Population Council, was 5 million.

If the population continues to expand at its present rate, Calcutta, India, will have a population of 66 million in the year 2000.

There are more Irish in New York City than in Dublin, more Italians in New York City than in Rome, and more Jews in New York City than in Tel Aviv.

It is estimated by the National Population Council that 74 billion human beings have been born and died in the last 500,000 years.

New York City has the largest black population of any city in the United States. It is followed by Chicago and Philadelphia.

Diet

Celery has negative calories—it takes more calories to eat a piece of celery than the celery has in it to begin with.

The candies most likely to cause tooth decay are dark

chocolate and fudge. Those least likely to damage the teeth are nut- or coconut-covered candies. The most harmful baked goods are chocolate-chip cookies, frosted cakes, and Graham crackers. The least harmful to the teeth are pies, plain cakes, and doughnuts.

One has to eat 11 pounds of potatoes to put on 1 pound of weight—a potato has no more calories than an apple. The potato was not known in Europe until the seventeenth century, when it was introduced by returning Spanish conquistadors. At first potatoes were thought disgusting and were blamed for starting outbreaks of leprosy and syphilis. As late as 1720 in America eating potatoes was believed to shorten a person's life.

The United States Postal Service assures its customers that they will not get fat licking stamps. There is no more than one-tenth of a calorie's worth of glue on every stamp.

Drugs

In 1865 opium was grown in the state of Virginia and a product was distilled from it that yielded 4 percent morphine. In 1867 it was grown in Tennessee; six years later it was cultivated in Kentucky. During these years opium, marijuana, and cocaine could be purchased legally over the counter from any druggist.

Cultivating opium poppies

In sixteenth-century Europe many druggists sold medicine made from the powder of Egyptian mummies. Such "medicine" was considered good for gout and catarrh and was often incorporated into products known as "mummy balm" or "Egyptian salve." In 1564 someone named Guy de la Fontaine attempted to corner the mummy market in Alexandria, a center for the export of such commodities. He discovered that Alexandrian merchants had for some time been selling the mummified remains of derelicts who had died not so long before from a variety of rather loathsome diseases.

In the Andes Mountains of Peru, where porters can work with superhuman endurance for days with little or no food by chewing the leaves of the coca plant (from which cocaine is extracted), distances are measured in *cocadas* rather than miles. A *cocada* is the span of road that can be traveled after chewing one portion of coca leaves.

The drug thiopentone can kill a human being in one second if injected directly into the blood.

Both George Washington and Thomas Jefferson grew *Cannabis sativa* (marijuana) on their plantations.

The Earth

The earth is estimated to be 4.5 billion years old. It travels through space at 660,000 miles per hour.

The oldest rocks in the world, the so-called St. Peter and St. Paul stones in the Atlantic Ocean, are 4 billion years old.

The earth weighs 6,588,000,000,000,000,000,000,000,000 tons.

The earth rotates on its axis more slowly in March than in September.

If the earth were compressed to a sphere with a 2-inch diameter, its surface would be as smooth as a billiard ball's.

The temperature of the earth's interior increases by 1 degree every 60 feet down.

If the world were to become totally flat and the oceans distributed themselves evenly over the earth's surface, the water would be approximately 2 miles deep at every point.

Glaciers occupy 5.8 million square miles, or 10 percent of the world's land surface, an area as large as South America.

The world is not round. It is an oblate spheroid, flattened at the poles and bulging at the equator.

Energy

The average American uses eight times as much fuel energy as an average person anywhere else in the world.

In one night, the World Trade Center in New York City uses more electricity than the entire city of Troy, New York.

A person uses more household energy shaving with a hand razor at a sink (because of the water power, the water pump, and so on) than he would by using an electric razor.

The world consumes 1 billion gallons of petroleum a day.

Petroleum accounts for half the world's energy supply.

One 75-watt bulb gives more light than three 25-watt bulbs.

Ten cords of wood stacked 4 feet wide by 4 feet high by 80 feet long have the same heating potential as 1,400 gallons of oil.

A car operates at maximum economy, gas-wise, at speeds between 25 and 35 miles per hour. A car that shifts manually gets 2 miles more per gallon of gas than a car with automatic shift. A car uses 1.6 ounces of gas idling for one minute. Half an ounce is used to start the average automobile.

Executions

In the Middle Ages animals were tried and publicly executed. Birds, wolves, insects, all were tried by ecclesiastical courts as witches and heretics, and suffered excommunication, torture, and death. The last such trial took place in 1740, when a French judge found a cow guilty of sorcery and ordered it hanged by the neck until dead. In 1386 at Falaise a judge ordered a pig to have its legs mutilated and then be hanged for killing a little girl. The pig was dressed up in the child's jacket and dragged to the town square with all the ceremony due a first-rate criminal. The execution, it is recorded, cost 6 sous plus a pair of gloves for the executioner so that he might carry out the killing with clean hands.

During the French revolution, a magistrate named Jean Baptiste Carrier, commissioner of the National Convention at Nantes, dispatched a number of boatloads of political prisoners into the Loire River. When the boat was in midstream he ordered a trap door in the bottom of the boat opened, sending an entire group of prisoners to their death. From his merciless methods of extermination the word *noyade,* meaning "mass drownings," was coined.

People condemned to the guillotine in France during the French revolution had the top of their head shaved. Two long locks of hair were left hanging at the temples.

Those condemned to die by the axe in medieval and Renaissance England were obliged to tip their executioner to ensure that he would complete the job in one blow. In some executions, notably that of Mary, Queen of Scots, it took fifteen whacks of the blade before the head was severed.

The Nazis used the guillotine to execute prisoners during World War II. Their version of the punishment had the condemned person lying on his back with his eyes forced open so that he had to watch the blade as it descended.

Beheading of
Mary, Queen of Scots

Until recent times, prisoners condemned to death in Mongolia were nailed into wooden boxes and left on the plains to die of exposure and starvation.

Fashion

Before King George IV of England ordered a set of boots made to fit each of his feet, shoes were designed to be worn on either foot.

In eighteenth-century England eyeglasses were often worn purely as fashionable accessories, not as aids to vision. Such glasses were frequently set in gold frames decorated with precious jewels. Sometimes the lenses were removed completely, leaving only the decorative frame to ornament the face.

Fashionable women in medieval Japan gilded or blackened their teeth. Today many Hindu women in India stain their teeth bright red to enhance their appearance.

The Maya Indians filed their front teeth to points and drilled holes in them so that they could be embellished with precious gems. They filled cavities in their teeth with pieces of jade.

The buttons on the back of a dress coat once served a purpose other than decoration. In seventeenth- and eighteenth-century Europe, the skirts of such coats were very long and the tails flapped about, interfering with movement. An ingenious gentleman had buttons sewn on the back so that when the wearer was in a hurry he could simply button up his skirts.

The pigtail worn for so many years by Chinese men was originally a symbol of abject humiliation. The Manchus, a tribe of Tartars, conquered China in 1644. To emphasize their suzerainty, they ordered each Chinese male to shave the forepart of his head and to permit the hair on the back

Chinese men at a fortuneteller's. All have shaved heads and pigtails.

of his head to grow long. This extended length of hair was then to be braided and tasseled, and in the presence of superiors always hung over the back. The pigtail, however, gradually became so popular among its wearers that in 1912 when the Manchus were defeated and dethroned, most Chinese men were loath to give it up.

The natives of Kandahar, Afghanistan, wear turbans which when unwrapped are 20 feet long.

A group of turbaned Afghan chiefs

Americans spend more than $125 billion a year on sneakers. One hundred million pairs were sold in 1975.

Kilts are not native to Scotland. They originated in France.

The shoestring was invented in England in 1790. Prior to this time all shoes were fastened with buckles.

In the late nineteenth century, it was the fashion among many English women to wear gold rings through their nipples. In an 1899 edition of the British journal *Society,* fascinating details are given about this peculiar fad. The woman who wished to wear such ornaments, the magazine said, had holes bored through her nipples and thin golden rings threaded through the holes. It was believed that wearing such rings made the breasts fuller and rounder, and that the rings were a stimulating sight for men when exposed. The operation was performed not by doctors, but by jewelers, much the way ear piercing is done today.

Firsts

Benjamin Franklin was the first head of the United States Post Office.

The first macaroni factory in the United States was established in 1848. It was started by Antoine Zegera in Brooklyn, New York.

The first United States Marine Corps officer of Chinese descent was commissioned in 1943. His name was Wilbur Sze. The first black to be commissioned in the Marines, John Rudder, received his commission in 1948.

The first telephone book ever issued contained only fifty names. It was published in New Haven, Connecticut, by the New Haven District Telephone Company in February, 1878.

King George VI of England became the first British monarch to set foot on American soil when he visited the World's Fair in New York City in 1939.

The first Secretary of Health, Education and Welfare was a

woman. Her name was Oveta Culp Hobby and she took office in 1953.

The Grand Canyon was not seen by a white man until after the Civil War. It was first entered on May 29, 1869, by the geologist John Wesley Powell.

Of the first five men to reach the North Pole, one was black, four were oriental, and one was white. The orientals were Eskimos serving as porters for their white leader, Robert Peary. The black was Matthew Henson, Peary's personal aide.

Wyoming was the first state to allow women to vote.

The Adventures of Tom Sawyer was the first novel ever to be written on a typewriter. It was typed on a Remington in 1875 by Mark Twain himself. Twain, however, wished to withhold the fact. He did not want to write testimonials, he said, or answer questions concerning the operation of the "newfangled thing."

Catherine de Medici was the first woman in Europe to use tobacco. She took it in a mixture of snuff.

The A & P was the first chain-store business to be established. It began in 1842.

Benjamin Franklin was America's first political cartoonist. His drawing of a snake divided into eight parts was published in Philadelphia in 1754.

Andrew Jackson was the first president to ride in a railroad train. The first to use a telephone was James Garfield. Theodore Roosevelt was the first president to ride in an automobile.

Theodore Roosevelt was the first United States president to visit a foreign country while in office. In November, 1906, he sailed on the U.S.S. *Louisiana* for Panama and Puerto Rico.

Fish

The teeth of the tiger shark rest on a spring. When the shark's mouth is closed, the teeth are pressed back firmly against the gums. When the mouth is opened, the teeth spring out, ready for action.

Head of tiger shark

The white shark (Carcharodon sp.):

has teeth that rank on a scale of hardness with steel.

is the only creature in the sea with no natural enemies; even killer whales normally avoid it.

can survive brain damage better than any animal in the world.

never gets sick. It has mysterious antibodies that give it immunity to practically every known bacterial invader. It is also one of the few animals known to be completely immune to cancer.

can hear sounds a mile away.

is always hungry; no matter how much it eats, its appetite is never satisfied—it lives in a state of continual hunger.

Despite their ferocity and reputation, however, sharks rarely attack man. Three times as many people are killed each year by lightning as are killed by sharks. A hundred more people die from bee stings each year than from shark bites.

The lanternfish has a glowing spot on the front of its head that acts like a miner's lamp when the fish is swimming in dark waters. This "lamp" is so powerful that it can shed light for a distance as great as 2 feet. Experiments have shown that when confined to an aquarium, the lanternfish can project enough light to allow a person to read a book in an otherwise totally darkened room.

Atlantic salmon are able to leap 15 feet high.

Most tropical marine fish could survive in a tank filled with human blood.

Minnows have teeth in their throat.

The lungfish can live out of water in a state of suspended animation for three years.

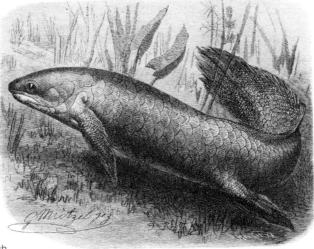

Lungfish

An electric eel can produce a shock of more than 600 volts, five times more powerful than a household outlet. It not only uses this power to kill its prey but to locate it as well—though it is born with eyes, it is blind as an adult and employs its electricity to find food in much the same way as man uses radar.

A marine catfish can taste with any part of its body. The female marine catfish hatches her eggs in her mouth.

The garfish has green bones.

The freshwater eel *(Anguilla rostrata* and *Anguilla anguilla):*

All freshwater eels, both the European and American species, are born in the same place, a seaweed- and vine-clogged section of the ocean south of Bermuda known as the Sargasso Sea. From this location, the eels migrate to

various parts of the world, the American eels to North America, the European eels to Europe. The trips may take as long as three years. Once they arrive at their destination, the males remain at the river mouths while the females move farther upstream, finally settling in small island lakes and ponds. They remain there for ten to fifteen years, until they receive a strange instinctive call back to the sea. Swimming against great river currents, leaping upward like salmon, sometimes leaving the water altogether to crawl along great stretches of land, the female eel finally makes her way back to the sea, where she joins the male. Then they swim together directly to the Sargasso Sea. Here they mate, spawn, and die.

Nasturtiums

Flowers, Plants, & Trees

The nasturtium derives its name from the Latin *nasus* ("nose") *tortum* ("to twist"). The flower's smell is so powerful that to inhale it was considered tantamount to having one's nose tweaked.

The Japanese have a special method for growing superb melons. They plant a seed, allow it to sprout and form buds, then pick all the buds but one. This one bud is allowed to mature into a full fruit. In this way a single fruit receives all the nutrients originally meant for the whole plant. The result is a remarkably succulent melon.

The cucumber is not a vegetable; botanically, it is a fruit. So are the eggplant, the pumpkin, the squash, the tomato, the gherkin, and the okra. Rhubarb, however, is botanically a vegetable, not a fruit.

Fruits and flowers of the cucumber plant

An orange tree may bear oranges for more than 100 years. The famous "Constable Tree," an orange tree brought to France in 1421, lived and bore fruit for 473 years.

Orange pickers

The General Sherman Tree in Sequoia National Park, California, is the largest tree in the world. It weighs more than 6,000 tons.

Poison oak is not oak; poison ivy is not ivy. Both are members of the cashew family (Anacardiaceae).

A peanut is not a nut. It is a legume.

The bark of the redwood tree is fireproof. Fires in redwood forests take place *inside* the trees.

Oak trees are struck by lightning more often than any other tree. This, it has been theorized, is one reason that the ancient Greeks considered oak trees sacred to Zeus, god of thunder and lightning.

The angle between the main branches of a tree and its trunk remains constant in each species—and this same angle is found between the principal vein of the tree's leaves and all its subsidiary branching veins.

Seedless oranges were not grown in the United States until 1871. The first ones came from Brazil and were planted in California.

The banana cannot reproduce itself. It can be propagated only by the hand of man. Further, the banana is not a tree,

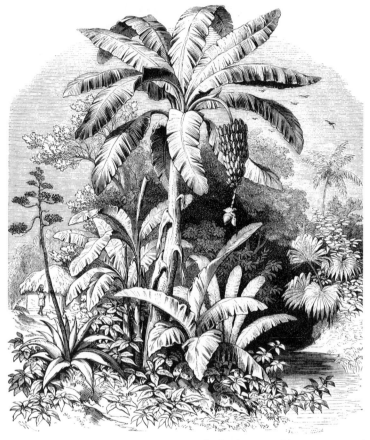

Right: Banana plant
Below: Leaves and fruit
of the baobab tree

it is an herb, the largest known of all plants without a woody stem or solid trunk.

The sequoias and redwoods of the American West Coast are *not* the oldest living trees in the world. The honor belongs to the macrozamia trees of Australia, which live 5,000 to 7,000 years and, some claim, may even reach 15,000 years.

The trunk of the African baobab tree is sometimes as wide as the tree is high. The tree is pollinated by bats, and its blossoms open only in moonlight.

The rings of a tree are always farther apart on the tree's southern side. Woodsmen often read tree rings to find the compass points.

Bamboo is not a tree. It is a wood grass.

The onion is a lily, botanically.

Cork comes from the bark of trees. Specifically, it is harvested from the cork tree, which takes more than ten years to produce one layer of cork.

Life preservers and the linings of aviators' jackets used during World War II were made from fiber found in milkweed pods.

In one day a full-grown oak tree expels 7 tons of water through its leaves.

During midsummer the radical leaves of the compass plant invariably point precisely north and south.

The orchid is named after the male genitalia. Its botanical family name, Orchidaceae, means "testicles" in Greek and may derive from an early notion that the orchid possessed aphrodisiac qualities.

The poinsettia flower is named after a nineteenth-century ambassador to Mexico, Joel R. Poinsett, who first brought the poinsettia plant to America.

The flower of the calla lily *(Amorphophallus titanum)* is 8 feet high and 12 feet wide. It is grown in Sumatra.

Eighty percent of the world's rose species come from Asia.

It takes 4,000 crocuses to produce a single ounce of saffron.

Bamboo and Rocks, detail of a 13th-century Chinese hanging scroll

Food & Drink

Diamond Jim Brady's average breakfast as recorded by a New York restauranteur: a gallon of orange juice, three eggs, a quarter of a loaf of corn bread, sirloin steak with fried potatoes, hominy grits and bacon, two muffins, and several pancakes. For dinner Diamond Jim might eat three dozen oysters, two bowls of turtle soup, and six crabs as an appetizer. Restaurant owners referred to him as the best twenty-five customers they ever had.

A raisin dropped in a glass of fresh champagne will bounce up and down continually from the bottom of the glass to the top.

In medieval England beer was often served with breakfast.

The United States Department of Agriculture reports that the average American eats 8½ pounds of pickles a year. Dill pickles are twice as popular as sweet.

Cabbage is 91 percent water.

Lettuce is the world's most popular green.

The term "cocktail" was invented in Elmsford, New York. A barmaid named Betsy Flanagan decorated her establishment with the tail feathers of cocks. One day a patron asked for "one of those cock tails." She served him a drink with a feather in it.

As many as 50 gallons of maple sap are needed to make a single gallon of maple sugar.

Dairy products account for 29 percent of all food consumed in the United States.

The Swedes drink more coffee than any other people in the world.

The pickle, an American favorite

Potato chips were invented by a black chef in Louisiana in 1865.

Goat's milk is used more widely throughout the world than cow's milk.

Milking goats in India

Wine tasters never drink the wine they taste. They sip it, swish it about, gargle it, and then spit it out. Swallowing wine is believed to dull the palate, not to mention the brain.

Wadakin and Matsuzuka beef, raised in Japan, are considered the two most tender kinds of beef in the world. The steers from which this meat is taken are isolated in totally dark stalls, fed on beer and beer mash, and hand-massaged by specially trained beef masseurs three times a day.

Wine will spoil if exposed to light; hence tinted bottles.

Chop suey was invented in the United States. Its creator was a Chinese dignitary visiting America in the nineteenth century. Requested by American friends to prepare an authentic Chinese meal and not having the proper ingredients, the Chinese gentleman ordered his cook to collect all available foods, pour them into a large pot, and flavor the whole thing with soya sauce, which was still relatively new and exotic to the western palate. Asked the name of this delicious concoction, the dignitary, spotting a pair of chopsticks lying near the bottle of soya sauce, replied, "Chop-soya." Through his heavy Chinese accent this became "chop suey," and so it has remained ever since.

Milk is heavier than cream.

According to the Nutritional Sciences Department of Cornell University, the best temperature at which to preserve frozen foods is 0° F (−18° C).

The purpose of the indentation at the bottom of a wine bottle is to strengthen the structure of the bottle and to trap the sediments in the wine.

Vintage port takes forty years to reach maturity.

The average person ingests about a ton of food and drink each year.

The age recorded on a whiskey bottle refers to the number of years it is aged *prior* to being bottled. Once in the bottle, whiskey does not improve.

Honey is the only food that does not spoil. Honey found in the tombs of Egyptian pharaohs has been tasted by archaeologists and found edible.

According to *Institutions/Volume Feeding* magazine, a trade journal for fast-food-chain operators, the single most popular entree in American restaurants is the hamburger. Right behind the hamburger are, in order, fried chicken, roast beef, spaghetti, turkey, baked ham, fried shrimp, and beef stew.

Haggis, a traditional Scottish dish, is made from the lungs, heart, and liver of a sheep, chopped with onions, seasonings, suet, and oatmeal, and then boiled in a bag made from the sheep's stomach.

More than one-third of the world's commercial supply of pineapples comes from Hawaii.

The strongest any liquor can be is 190 proof. This means the beverage is a little more than 97 percent alcohol.

Argentinians eat more meat than any other nation in the world—an average of 10 ounces per person per day.

The herring is the most widely eaten fish in the world. Nutritionally its fuel value is equal to that of a beefsteak.

The custom of serving a slice of lemon with fish dates back to the Middle Ages; the lemon was originally intended for remedial purposes rather than to flavor the fish. It was believed that if a person accidentally swallowed a fish bone, the lemon juice would dissolve it.

Americans spend $600 million a year on hot dogs. They consume enough of them each year to form a chain stretching from the earth to the moon and back again. The average American eats forty hot dogs a year. But the hot dog is not an American invention; it was first produced in Germany in 1852 by a group of butchers in Frankfurt.

There are professional tea tasters as well as wine tasters.

Tea tasters at work in
New York, 1883

In Wilton, Maine, there is a cannery that imports and cans only dandelion greens.

A hard-boiled egg will spin. An uncooked or soft-boiled egg will not.

Gambling

From a fifty-two-card deck it is possible to deal 2,598,960 different five-card poker hands. Of these 1,088,240 will contain a pair. Other possibilities are 4 royal flushes, 36 straight flushes, 624 four-of-a-kind hands, 3,744 full houses, 5,108 flushes, 10,200 straights, 54,912 three-of-a-kind hands, and 123,552 two-pair hands.

Gamblers in ancient Greece made dice from the anklebones and shoulder blades of sheep.

Eskimos don't gamble.

At race tracks, the favorite wins fewer than 30 percent of all horse races.

The opposite sides of a dice cube always add up to seven.

Horse-racing regulations state that no race horse's name may contain more than eighteen letters. (Names that are too long would be cumbersome on racing sheets.) Apostrophes, hyphens, and spaces between words count as letters.

THE FINISH

According to *Gambler's Digest,* more cheating takes place in private, friendly gambling games than in all other gambling games combined.

The Card Players, by Lucas van Leyden

There is one slot machine in Las Vegas for every eight inhabitants.

Sir Miles Partridge once played at dice with Henry VIII for the bells of St. Paul's church, won, and collected the bells.

On a bingo card of ninety numbers there are approximately 44 million possible ways to make bingo.

Madame de Montespan, second wife of Louis XIV, once lost 4 million francs in a half-hour at the gambling table.

In 1950 at the Las Vegas Desert Inn, an anonymous sailor made twenty-seven straight passes (wins) with the dice at craps. The odds against such a feat are 12,467,890 to 1. Had he bet the house limit on each roll he would have earned $268 million. As it was, he was so timid with his wagers that he walked away from the table with only $750. The dice today are enshrined in the hotel on a velvet pillow under glass.

Residents of Nevada bet an average of $846 a year in gambling casinos.

When prevented from gambling, compulsive gamblers often experience physical withdrawal symptoms resembling those undergone by heroin addicts. The reactions range from restlessness to shakiness, severe headaches, and diarrhea.

In eighteenth-century English gambling dens, there was an employee whose only job was to swallow the dice if there was a police raid.

At Brook's, an eighteenth-century English gambling club, the faro table had a large semicircular section cut out of one of its sides in order to accommodate the enormous stomach of the famous statesman Charles James Fox.

There are no clocks in Las Vegas gambling casinos.

In poker a pair of aces and a pair of eights is known as a "dead man's hand." The odd name originated in 1876,

Jack McCall shooting
Wild Bill Hickok, 1876

when Wild Bill Hickok was shot down by Jack McCall during a card game in a saloon in Deadwood, South Dakota. As Wild Bill slumped over the table he exposed his hand for all to see—it showed a pair of eights and a pair of aces.

The receipts from illegal gambling each year in the United States surpass the total revenues of America's seventy-five largest industrial organizations combined.

According to *Gambler's Digest,* an estimated $1 million is lost at race tracks each year by people who lose or carelessly throw away winning tickets.

No patent can ever be taken out on a gambling machine in the United States.

Parimutuel betting was invented in 1865 by a Parisian perfume maker named Pierre Oller.

Games & Hobbies

The game of billiards was popularized in France by Louis XIV. The King started playing the game at the recommendation of his physicians. The constant stretching exercise

Louis XIV
at a game of billiards

Louis received in playing billiards, his physicians believed, would relieve him of his digestive problems.

Modern playing cards were derived from the tarot fortune-telling deck. The original tarot was divided into two sections, the major arcane (dropped from the modern deck) and the minor arcane. The minor arcane was composed of four suits: cups, wands, coins, and swords. In the modern deck these became the hearts, clubs, diamonds, and spades. Similarly, the early tarot had kings, queens, and knights (jacks), plus a page who has been eliminated from contemporary decks.

There are 170,000,000,000,000,000,000,000,000 ways to play the ten opening moves in a game of chess.

The children's game "Ring Around the Rosy" and the words that accompany it ("Ring around the rosy, pocket full of posy, ashes, ashes, all fall down") derive from the medieval practice of scattering rose petals in a circle around one's bed ("ring around the rosy") and carrying small bouquets ("pocket full of posy") as protection against the Black Plague ("all fall down").

Benjamin Franklin was one of the first people to manufacture playing cards in America.

The game of dominoes was invented by French monks. It is named for a phrase in the Vesper services: *Dixit Dominus Domineo Meo.*

Stamp collecting is the most popular hobby in the world.

During the French revolution, because they smacked of royalist influence, kings, queens, and jacks were removed from the standard deck of cards and were replaced by "liberty" (queens), "nature" (kings), and "virtue" (jacks). The hearts, clubs, spades, and diamonds were changed to peace, war, art, and commerce.

There are playing cards manufactured especially for left-handed people. Normally the pips on a card are in the upper left-hand corner and lower right for the convenience of right-handed fanners. Left-handed playing cards have pips on all four corners.

The practice of using ten pins in the game of bowling originated in colonial America as a means of circumventing a gaming law. An eighteenth-century ordinance in Connecticut ruled that "bowling at nine pins" was illegal, and offenders were often jailed or placed in stocks. To get around this law, bowlers added an extra pin to the game, so that they would be playing "ten pins" rather than "nine pins." The name stuck, and so did the number of pins.

A game of bowls

Geography

The principality of Monaco consists of only 370 acres.

More than 25 percent of the world's forests are in Siberia.

The United States would fit into the continent of Africa three and a half times.

The Sahara Desert comprises an area as large as Europe. Its total land mass is some 3,565,565 square miles.

All continents, with the exception of Antarctica, are wider in the north than in the south.

Florida is *not* the southernmost state in the United States. Hawaii is farther south.

The town of Hamilton, Ontario, Canada, is closer to the equator than it is to the North Pole.

More than two-thirds of the earth's land surface lies north of the equator.

Of the 3,000 islands in the Bahama chain in the Caribbean, only 20 are inhabited.

Israel is one-quarter the size of the state of Maine.

The precise geographical center of the North American continent is in a town called Rugby, North Dakota.

There are sand dunes in Arcachon, France, that are 350 feet high.

Panama (because of a bend in the isthmus) is the only place in the world where one can see the sun rise on the Pacific Ocean and set on the Atlantic.

For 186 days a year the sun is not seen at the North Pole.

The Hawaiian Islands are the projecting tops of the biggest mountain range in the world. Mauna Kea, on the island of Hawaii and part of this range, is the largest mountain on earth—though partially submerged, its full height from base to crown is 33,476 feet, some 4,000 feet taller than Mount Everest.

The distance from Honolulu to New York is greater than the distance from Honolulu to Japan.

Saudi Arabia, which contains one of the largest expanses of desert in the world and through which great camel caravans have traveled for centuries, must import both sand and camels. River sand is sent to Arabia by the ton from Scotland for use in construction; desert sands are not suitable for building purposes. And since camel herds are dwindling in Arabia, camels must be imported from North Africa.

Jacksonville, Florida, has the largest total area of any city in the United States. It takes in 460 square miles, almost twice the area of Los Angeles.

Question: If one were to drive from Los Angeles, California, to Reno, Nevada, in which direction would he be going, east or west? *Answer:* West. (Check the map.)

In the Northern Hemisphere water goes down drains counterclockwise. In the Southern Hemisphere it goes down clockwise.

The King Ranch in Texas is bigger than the state of Rhode Island. It comprises 1.25 million acres and was the first ranch in the world to be completely fenced in. At one time its borders were guarded by armed patrol.

Insects & Spiders

The female praying mantis devours the male while they are mating. The male sometimes continues copulating even after the female has bitten off his head and part of his upper torso!

A male spider's penis is located at the end of one of its legs.

Ants keep slaves. Certain species, the so-called sanguinary ants in particular, raid the nests of other ant tribes, kill the queen, and kidnap many of the workers. The workers are brought back to the captors' hive, where they are coerced into performing menial tasks.

A house fly lives only two weeks.

Every night, wasps bite into the stem of a plant, lock their mandibles into position, stretch out at right angles to the stem, and, with legs dangling, fall asleep.

Digger wasp, with cocoon and larva

In rainy climates, some breeds of termites attach special overhanging eaves to their nests. These eaves deflect downpours and keep the nests dry. The compass termite, an Australian breed, builds its nest in the shape of an axe head, the sides of which always point north and south. African termites in search of water will bore holes as deep as 130 feet into the earth until they find the water table.

After mating, the female black widow spider turns on her partner and devours him. The female may dispatch as many as twenty-five suitors a day in this manner.

Termites are not related to ants. They are part of the cockroach family.

In a beehive, only 1½ ounces of wax are used to build a comb that will hold 4 pounds of honey.

Constructing a honeycomb

Queen termites may live for fifty years.

The Mexican fishing spider attaches itself to a small leaf, floats across a pond as if on a raft, and from this vantage point hunts its prey, large tadpoles and small fish.

According to the United States Department of Agriculture, the best time to spray household insects is 4:00 P.M. Insects are most active and vulnerable at this time.

Only female bees work. Males remain in the hive and literally do nothing, their only mission in life being to fertilize the queen bee on her maiden flight. For this purpose literally

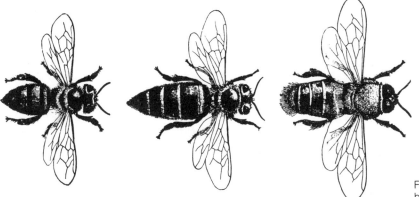

From left: Worker, queen bee, and male (drone)

thousands of males are hatched, out of which only one or two mate with the queen. After they have served their function, the males are not allowed back into the hive but are left outside, where they starve to death.

Flies prefer to breed in the center of a room. This is why experts advise placing flypaper away from corners.

Cockroaches have lived on the earth for 250 million years without changing in any way whatsoever.

The caterpillar has more than 2,000 muscles.

Spiders never spin webs in structures made of chestnut wood. That is why so many European châteaux were built with chestnut beams—spider webs on a 50-foot beamed ceiling can be difficult to clean!

The reason a fly swatter is an efficient tool for killing flies while the human hand is not is as follows: a fly's tactile sense is controlled by numerous sensory hairs covering its entire body. These hairs are especially sensitive to air pressure. The movement of a hand or any other solid object creates fluctuations of air and warns the fly well in advance of the blow. The fly swatter, however, has many holes arranged along its surface, so that it displaces little air as it bears down on its victim. Thus the fly is caught unawares.

The deer botfly can fly faster than a jet plane. It has been clocked at a speed of 818 miles per hour. It crosses 400 yards in one second and moves 13 miles in a minute. The deer botfly flies so fast that it is almost invisible to the human eye.

There are more beetles on earth than any other living creature. The number of *species alone* is nearly a quarter-million (the United States has 28,000 species).

A grasshopper can leap over obstacles 500 times its own height. In relation to its size, it has the greatest jumping ability of all animals.

An ant can lift 50 times its own weight. A bee can handle 300 times its own weight, which is equivalent to a human being pulling a 10-ton trailer.

There are 5 million different species of insects in the world. The insect population of the world is at least 1,000,000,000,000,000,000. The weight of the world's insect population exceeds that of man by a factor of twelve.

The animal with the largest brain in proportion to its body size is the ant.

The honeybee kills more people each year world-wide than poisonous snakes.

Bees can see ultraviolet light.

Butterflies taste with their hind feet.

There are more than 100,000 different species of butterflies.

The leaf-cutter ant sometimes makes anthills 16 feet deep and an acre wide.

If one places a minute amount of liquor on a scorpion, it will instantly go mad and sting itself to death.

Only female mosquitoes bite.

A flea can jump 200 times the length of its own body. This is equivalent to a person jumping almost a quarter of a mile.

Mosquitoes are attracted to the color blue twice as much as to any other color.

A male emperor moth can detect and find a female of his species a mile away.

It would take 27,000 spiders, each spinning a single web, to produce a pound of web.

Bees have five eyes. There are three small eyes on the top of a bee's head and two larger ones in front.

A queen bee may lay as many as 3,000 eggs in a single day.

Ants stretch when they wake up. They also appear to yawn in a very human manner before taking up the tasks of the day.

In September, 1951, seventeen-month-old Mark Bennet of Vancouver, B.C., was stung 447 times by wasps and lived. He was released from the hospital after twenty days of treatment.

A cockroach can live several weeks with its head cut off.

The common house fly, *Musca domestica,* cannot survive in Alaska. It is too cold. Those that do appear there are brought in by boat or plane and perish without reproducing. Mosquitoes, on the other hand, love cold weather. Specimens have been found near the North Pole.

The bumblebee does not die when it stings—it can sting again and again. In bumblebee hives, the entire colony, except for the queen, dies at the end of each summer. Each year an entirely new colony of bees must be produced.

Cicadas have their hearing organs in their stomachs, at the base of the abdomen. Crickets have their hearing organs in their knees, or, more precisely, in the oval slits of their forelegs.

The bombardier beetle, when disturbed, defends itself by emitting a series of explosions, sometimes setting off four or five reports in succession. The noises sound like miniature popgun blasts and are accompanied by a cloud of reddish-colored, vile-smelling fluid.

Inventions

Orson S. Fowler, who in the mid-nineteenth century popularized the science of phrenology, was also the inventor of the octagon house, an eight-sided dwelling that enjoyed great popularity in America from the 1840's through the 1860's.

The first plastic ever invented was celluloid, which is still used to make billiard balls. It came into use in 1868, when cellulose nitrate was first combined with natural camphor in a laboratory. At the time it was regarded as a mere curiosity.

As of 1940, a total of ninety-four patents had been taken out on shaving mugs.

The Chinese invented the speedometer. In 1027 Lu Tao-lung presented the Emperor Jen Chung with a cart that could measure the distances it spanned by means of a mechanism with eight wheels and two moving arms. One arm struck a drum each time a *li* (about a third of a mile) was covered. Another rang a bell every 10 *li*.

The rickshaw was invented by an American. The Reverend Jonathan Scobie, a Baptist minister living in Yokohama, Ja-

pan, built the first model in 1869 in order to transport his invalid wife through the city streets. Copies were made by the minister's parishioners and soon the rickshaw became a standard mode of transportation in the Orient.

In 1875 the director of the United States Patent Office sent in his resignation and advised that his department be closed. There was nothing left to invent, he claimed.

Thomas Jefferson invented the dumbwaiter.

The telephone was not invented by Alexander Graham Bell. Its first creator was a German, Philip Reis, who in 1861 made a primitive sending-receiving transmitter which he called the "telephone." Twelve years later Elisha Gray of Chicago completed a short-distance telephone communication. Bell's invention, patented in March, 1876, was distinguished by the fact that it was the first sending-receiving mechanism over which the human voice could be transmitted.

The postage stamp was invented by an Englishman named James Chambers in 1834. Before that time envelopes had stamps engraved upon them. They were bulky, however, and Chambers' invention caught on immediately. Postage stamps were introduced to America in 1847.

James Ramsey invented a steam-driven motorboat in 1784. He ran it on the Potomac River, and the event was witnessed by George Washington.

Benjamin Franklin invented crop insurance.

Henry Ford did not invent the automobile. It was the invention of several nineteenth-century engineers, paramount among them being two Germans, Gottlieb Daimler and Karl Benz. What Ford did was to mass-produce automobiles and provide cheap service for them.

The parachute was invented more than a hundred years before the airplane. It was the creation of a Frenchman,

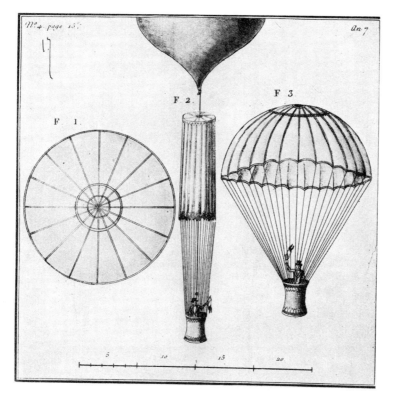

Early French parachute

Louis Lenormand, who designed it in 1783 to save people who had to jump from burning buildings. In 1797 Jacques Garnerin gave a public exhibition of parachuting, descending 3,000 feet from a balloon.

Roulette was invented by the great French mathematician and philosopher Blaise Pascal. It was a by-product of his experiments with perpetual motion.

The parking meter was invented in Oklahoma City. It was the brainstorm of one Carl Magee, whose first model appeared in 1935. Early models look almost exactly like modern ones: few items have changed as little through the years as the parking meter.

James J. Ritty, owner of a tavern in Dayton, Ohio, invented the cash register in 1879 to stop his patrons from pilfering house profits.

Joseph Priestley, the English chemist, invented carbonated water. It was a by-product of his investigations into the chemistry of air.

The monkey wrench is named after its inventor, a London blacksmith named Charles Moncke.

Camel's-hair brushes are not made of camel's hair. They were invented by a man named Mr. Camel.

Wallpaper was invented in Philadelphia. The inventor was one Plunket Fleeson, who in 1739 stamped designs on paper with woodblocks and painted them in by hand. In August of that year Fleeson advertised in the Pennsylvania *Gazette* the sale of "bedticks, choice live geese feathers, as well as paper hangings."

Leonardo da Vinci invented the scissors.

Language

To "decimate" does not mean to obliterate or wipe out. It means to destroy one-tenth of something. Originally the word referred to a Roman military tradition in which an entire troop would be punished for disobedience by decimation, that is, by the killing of every tenth man. There are accounts of this form of punishment being used in the English and French armies up to the time of World War I.

In Middle English the word "minister" meant "lowly person." It was originally adopted as a term of humility for men of the church.

The term "hooker," meaning a prostitute, originated with U.S. Army General Joseph Hooker, whose penchant for war was matched only by his predilection for paid female companionship. In New Orleans during the Civil War, Hooker spent so much time frolicking with ladies of the night that the women came to be called "Hooker's division." Eventually these specialized "troops" became known simply as "hookers."

The original name for the butterfly was "flutterby."

In the vast majority of the world's languages, the word for "mother" begins with the letter M.

"Facetious" and "abstemious" are the only two words in the English language that contain the vowels *a, e, i, o,* and *u* in their proper order.

The word "live" spelled backward is "evil."

Eskimos have more than twenty words to describe snow.

What is called a "French kiss" in England and America is known as an "English kiss" in France.

The Kiss, by
Constantin Brancusi

The most commonly used word in English conversation is "I."

The act of snapping one's fingers has a name. It is called a "fillip."

The language of Taki, spoken in parts of French Guinea, consists of only 340 words.

The words CHOICE COD read the same when held in front of a mirror upside-down.

Words that are really words:

bezel—the edge of a cutting tool.

callithump—a loud parade.

clerihew—a light satirical four-line verse containing specific reference to a person, invented by E. Clerihew Bentley (1875–1956). Clerihew wrote his first clerihew while still in school:

> Sir Humphry Davy
> Abominated gravy.
> He lived in the odium
> Of having discovered sodium.

googol—the figure 1 followed by 100 zeros.

haruspex—an ancient Roman priest who practiced fortunetelling by reading entrails of sacrificed animals.

hendecasyllabic—an adjective applied to a line of verse of eleven syllables.

pneumoultramicroscopicsilicovolcanoconiosis—a disease of the lungs developed by coal miners from breathing underground fumes.

pseudepigrapha—spurious writings, particularly those attributed to Biblical sources.

scop—an Old English poet.

A "clue" originally meant a ball of thread. This is why one is said to "unravel" the clues of a mystery.

The ampersand (&) was once a letter of the English alphabet.

The word "gas," coined by the chemist J. B. van Helmont, is taken from the word *chaos,* which means "unformed" in Greek.

The words "naked" and "nude" are *not* the same. Naked implies unprotected. Nude means unclothed.

La Grande Odalisque, by Jean Auguste Dominique Ingres

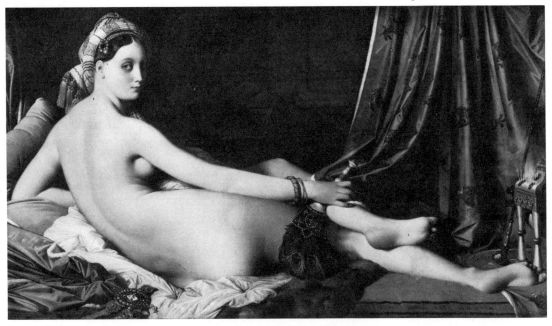

The word "geriatrics" was not coined until 1951.

In Elizabethan slang the term "to die" meant to have an orgasm. This double entendre was often used by John Donne *(The Prohibition, The Canonization),* and by Shakespeare in *King Lear*.

The word "toast," meaning a proposal of health, originated in Rome, where an actual bit of spiced, burned bread was dropped into wine to improve the drink's flavor, absorb its sediment, and thus make it more healthful.

General Jackson and His Lady sharing a toast, watercolor by H. Young

The word "turnpike" originated in the days when toll collectors were armed with pikes, long-handled weapons with sharp iron heads. They used these weapons to prevent travelers who refused to pay the tariff from using their roads.

E is the most frequently used letter in the English alphabet, Q the least.

The word "bamboo" has contributed two colloquialisms to the English language. First, we owe to it the word "joint," meaning a disreputable gathering place, a dive. This is because the pipes used in opium dens were crafted of bamboo and had many "joints." (It has been suggested that marijuana cigarettes are also known as "joints" because of their association with opium dens.) Second, there is the word "bamboozle," which means to fool or cheat. This

Opium den in New York, 1881

traces back to the Chinese custom of punishing swindlers by whacking them on the hands and back with bamboo poles. Any smart aleck so treated was a "bamboozler," that is, one worthy of being tanned with bamboo.

The word "clodhopper" originated in early England as a term of derision for the peasantry. In those days farmers traveled by foot, and had to step or jump across clods of plowed earth. Unlike the gentry, who traveled by carriage or by steed, the peasants were therefore "clodhoppers"—those who had to hop over clods.

The word "queue" is the only word in the English language that is still pronounced the same way when the last four letters are removed.

When sailors speak of sheets (as in "four sheets to the wind") they are not talking about sails. A sheet in nautical terminology is a rope or chain.

The jackrabbit is not a rabbit; it is a hare. A Jerusalem artichoke is not an artichoke; it is a sunflower. Arabic numerals are not Arabic; they were invented in India. India ink (sometimes called "Chinese ink") was not known until recently in either China or India.

The word "tip," meaning a gratuity, was originally an acronym standing for "To Insure Promptness."

The word "robot" was coined in 1920 in a play, *R.U.R.* (the initials stood for Rossum's Universal Robots), written by the Czech dramatist Karel Capek.

Question: What is unusual about the sentence "Jackdaws love my big sphinx of quartz"? *Answer:* It is the shortest English sentence yet devised to include all the letters of the alphabet.

Rhubarb is named after the Volga River. In Greek the name of the Volga is *Rha,* and *barb* means "uncultivated." Rhubarb is thus a wild plant that grows along the Volga.

Cinderella's slipper, many scholars believe, was made of fur, not glass. The word *verre,* or "glass," they claim, was incorrectly substituted in early versions of the story for the word *vaire.* In medieval French, *vaire* means "fur."

The word "toady" originally referred to a magician's assistant who literally ate toads as part of the show. Toads, at one time, were thought to be poisonous; when the "toady" recovered from eating one of them, it was considered an indication of the magician's great power.

The term "freelance" was invented by Sir Walter Scott to refer to itinerant mercenary soldiers who sold their abilities to the highest bidder. At first such soldiers were known as "free companions." Since they usually traveled with their own weapons, including lances, Scott dubbed them "free lancers."

The letter B took its present form from a symbol used in Egyptian hieroglyphics to represent a house. Its original Egyptian form looked very much like its modern one.

The word "Mikado" did not refer to the Japanese emperor himself but to the door of his royal chamber. In medieval Japan it was considered in bad taste to speak of this great personage directly, so instead his existence was inferred by referring to the entrance to his place of residence.

A fireplace is called a "mantelpiece" because at one time people hung their coats (or "mantles") over the fireplace to dry them.

In England, corn means wheat. In the Bible, corn means grain.

Laws

Prior to the adoption of the Twelfth Amendment in 1804, the candidate who ran second in a presidential race automatically became vice-president. Thomas Jefferson became John Adams' vice-president in this way.

In Turkey, in the sixteenth and seventeenth centuries, anyone caught drinking coffee was put to death.

The United States Supreme Court once ruled Federal income tax unconstitutional. Income tax was first imposed during the Civil War as a temporary revenue-raising measure. In the late 1800's the government attempted to revive the levy again, but the Supreme Court ruled it in violation of the constitutional provision that direct taxes must be apportioned among the states according to their population. In 1913, however, Congress passed the Sixteenth Amendment, making a Federal impost legal once again.

It is illegal to hunt camels in the state of Arizona.

American Indians do not have to pay tax on their land.

Connecticut and Rhode Island never ratified the 18th Amendment (Prohibition).

In seventeenth-century Japan, no citizen was allowed to leave the country on penalty of death. Anyone caught coming or going without permission was executed on the spot.

Before 1941 fingerprints were not accepted as evidence in court. Up to that time it was not an established fact that no two fingerprints were alike. Today the only way in which fingerprints will *not* be allowed as evidence is if the defense can prove that there are in fact two sets of fingerprints somewhere in the world that match.

New York was the first state to require the licensing of motor vehicles. The law was adopted in 1901.

Until 1893, lynching was legal in the United States. The first antilynching law was passed in Georgia, but it only made the violation punishable by four years in prison.

Cattle branding in the United States did not originate in the West. It began in Connecticut in the mid-nineteenth century, when farmers were required by law to mark all their pigs.

During the time of Peter the Great, any Russian man who wore a beard was required to pay a special tax.

Literature

Voltaire considered Shakespeare's works so deplorable that he referred to the Bard as "that drunken fool."

All the proceeds earned from James M. Barrie's book *Peter Pan* were bequeathed to the Great Ormond Street Hospital for Sick Children in London.

Marcel Proust's *Remembrance of Things Past* contains almost 1.5 million words.

Fagin, the sinister villain in Charles Dickens' *Oliver Twist,* was also the name of Dickens' best friend, Bob Fagin.

Emily Dickinson wrote more than nine hundred poems, only four of which were published during her lifetime.

Gibbon spent twenty years writing *The Decline and Fall of the Roman Empire.* Noah Webster spent thirty-six years writing his dictionary.

The Indian epic poem the *Mahabhrata* is eight times longer than the *Iliad* and the *Odyssey* combined.

There is no living descendant of William Shakespeare.

The great English poet John Keats died at the age of twenty-six.

Alfred, Lord Tennyson wrote a 6,000-word epic poem when he was twelve years old.

Robert Louis Stevenson said that he had envisioned the entire story of *Dr. Jekyll and Mr. Hyde* in a dream and simply recorded it the way he saw it. Stevenson claimed to be able to dream plots for his stories at will.

John Bunyan, author of *Pilgrim's Progress,* wrote most of

his famous book while in jail. He was imprisoned for twelve years for preaching without a license.

The original story of *Alice in Wonderland* was not known as *Alice in Wonderland* at all. It was called *Alice's Adventures Under Ground* and was illustrated by the author himself, Lewis Carroll—whose name was not Lewis Carroll, but Charles Lutwidge Dodgson. Dodgson was a mathematics professor at Christ's Church, Oxford.

Left: Illustration from *Alice in Wonderland*
Below: William Cullen Bryant

In James M. Barrie's *Peter Pan,* the place where children go with Peter Pan is not called "Never-Never Land." It is called "Neverland."

The fairy tales "Puss in Boots," "Little Red Ridinghood," "Cinderella," and many others were first written down by Charles Perrault, who also helped design part of the Louvre.

Shakespeare once wrote a play called *What You Will.* (Its alternate title: *Twelfth Night.*)

William Cullen Bryant, famous American critic, biographer, and civic leader, published a well-known satire on Thomas Jefferson at the age of thirteen. Before he was eighteen he had written his most famous poem, "To a Waterfowl."

In *Gulliver's Travels* Jonathan Swift described the two

moons of Mars, Phobos and Deimos, giving their exact size and speeds of rotation. He did this more than a hundred years before either moon was discovered.

Alexander Pope published "The Rape of the Lock" at age twenty-four. Browning wrote "Pauline" when he was twenty. Byron wrote "Childe Harold" at twenty-four. Keats wrote "Endymion" at twenty-three.

The wife of the poet Percy Bysshe Shelley was the creator of the Frankenstein story. Mary Wollstonecraft Shelley wrote the book *Frankenstein* in 1818, basing it on the writings of certain alchemists who claimed to have created a tiny human being, called a homunculus, in a test tube.

Treasure Island was created by Robert Louis Stevenson on a lark. Drawing a treasure map for his stepson on a rainy day, Stevenson was urged by the child to make up stories to go along with the drawings. Stevenson liked the stories so much he wrote them down, and these became the basis for his great novel.

Illustration from
Treasure Island, by
Howard Pyle

After completing his book on the French revolution, the great English historian Thomas Carlyle gave the manuscript to his friend John Stuart Mill to proofread. By mistake Mill's housemaid used the papers to kindle a fire and destroyed the entire manuscript. Undaunted, Carlyle sat down and, without benefit of notes (he had destroyed these himself), completely reconstructed and rewrote the book.

Thomas Carlyle

Edgar Allan Poe invented the detective story. Before he wrote "The Murders in the Rue Morgue" and "The Mystery of Marie Roget" the genre was totally unknown in English or American literature.

Samuel Taylor Coleridge wrote his famous poem "Kubla Khan" directly from a dream. Coleridge was in the midst of writing down the visions he had seen in this dream when someone knocked on the door and he rose to let him in. On returning to his work, Coleridge found that he could not remember the rest of the dream. That is why "Kubla Khan" remains unfinished.

The original title of Jane Austen's novel *Pride and Prejudice* was *First Impressions.*

Magic & the Occult

Bobbing for apples at Halloween originated as part of a divinatory technique practiced by the Druids. Participants floated apples in a tub of water on the 31st of October (the Druid New Year's Eve) and attempted to fish them out without using their hands. Those who succeeded were guaranteed a prosperous year.

Magical symbols drawn by Roman soldiers on shields to repel the evil eye became the basis for European heraldic designs during the Middle Ages.

The Three Kings of the Nativity story were actually sorcerers. They were magicians, priests of the Zoroastrian religion of Persia. The word "magi" (as in the Three Magi) is the plural of *magus*, meaning "wizard" in Old Persian. It is from this root that the word "magic" is derived.

Adoration of the Magi,
engraving by P. Beljembe

Some occult tongue-twisters:

Alextoromantia: Divination based on the direction in which a rooster turns when let loose in a circle.

Alextryomancy: Divination by reading the random configurations formed by scattering grains of wheat on the ground.

Amniomancy: Foretelling a child's future from the arrangement of the amniotic membrane at the child's birth.

Arithomancy: Divination by abstruse and secret numerical calculations.

Belomancy: Divination by reading the flight patterns of randomly shot arrows and their position when they land.

Cereoscopy: Interpreting the patterns made by wax melted in boiling water.

Cledonism: Finding omens in the first words one hears upon rising in the morning.

Hydroscopy: Divination by reading the ripples created by three stones tossed into a pond.

Kieidiscopy: Divination by reading the undulations of a key swinging on a string.

Lycanthropy: The study of werewolves.

Metoposcopy: Divination by reading the positions, shapes, and sizes of the moles or blemishes on a person's body.

Ornithomancy: Divination by reading the flight patterns of birds.

Pyromancy: Divination by reading the movements of a flame.

Rhabdomancy: Hunting for gold, water, or precious metals by using a hazel wand as a pointer.

Scapulomancy: Divination by reading the cracks and fissures in the roasted shoulder bones of a sheep.

Screeology: The art of reading the future in a crystal ball.

Manners & Customs

In ancient Japan public contests were held to see who in a town could break wind loudest and longest. Winners were awarded many prizes and received great acclaim.

The pilgrims in Massachusetts used a special tool in church, a wooden ball attached to a long string on a stick. If anyone fell asleep during a sermon (which might go on for seven or eight hours) a specially appointed member of the clergy would hoist the pole over the reprobate's head and clop him with the wooden ball.

When ancient Egyptian priests held a banquet, a large mummy was often carried into the feast chamber and propped up at the table where all the priests could see it, a reminder that even while at pleasure, death was ever near.

The ancient Egyptians slept on pillows made of stone.

In medieval China and parts of Africa one method of enforcing chastity was to sew up a girl's vaginal labia as soon as she reached puberty. The stitches were not cut until marriage; the husband then had the option of sewing them up again if he was called to war or on a long journey.

In Elizabethan England the spoon was such a novelty, such a prized rarity, that people carried their own folding spoons to banquets.

Tibetans drink tea made of salt and rancid yak butter. Tibetan women carry a special instrument with metal blades for cleaning their ears and picking their nose.

Date-palm trees in Iraq are passed down through generations as part of family legacies. The trees are given individual names, have carefully recorded personal histories, and are considered a basic part of family wealth.

The champagne used to christen a ship is a substitute for human blood. In bygone times the Vikings and various South Sea tribes sacrificed human beings on the prows of their ships so that the spirits of the murdered victims would guard the craft. Later wine was substituted for blood, and, in our day, champagne for wine.

During the Middle Ages German men went to the barber to take a bath as well as to get a shave.

At Versailles, during the reign of Louis XIV, it was considered gauche to knock on a door with the knuckles. Instead one scratched with the little finger of the left hand,

and for this purpose courtiers let that particular nail grow long.

America in the year 1800:

There was no public library.

Crockery plates were objected to because they dulled knives.

Over one-fifth of the country's population lived in the state of Virginia.

Men and women spat on the floors of their own homes and bathed only once a week.

When someone was finished with dinner he placed his spoon across his cup to show that he wanted no more food.

Gentlemen wore wigs and powdered their hair.

When gentlemen in medieval Japan wished to seal an agreement, they urinated together, crisscrossing their streams of urine.

Among the Betsileo natives of Madagascar, in the eighteenth century, there was a caste of servants known as the *ramanga* who were made to eat all nail parings and blood lost by members of the upper classes. If the nail parings were too long or jagged they were minced up before being gobbled down. If a noble cut himself or was wounded in battle a *ramanga* would lick his wounds. Those of high rank rarely went anywhere without these attendants, and if by chance a nail broke or blood flowed when the aristocrat was alone he would preserve the residues and later give them to a *ramanga,* who obediently swallowed them.

In medieval Japan, a woman who was caught alone in a room with a man other than her husband was immediately put to death, even if the meeting was completely innocent.

The Tasaday tribe recently discovered in the Philippine Islands has no known enemies, no weapons of war, no words in their language for hate, war or dislike. They neither hunt nor cultivate.

In medieval Spain it was customary to clean the teeth with

stale urine. The theory behind this strange practice was that the urine would render the teeth especially bright and keep them firmly fixed in the gums.

Marriage & Divorce

According to the Population Council, people overwhelmingly tend to marry partners who live near them.

It takes one day to get a divorce in the Dominican Republic.

Mathematics & Numbers

George Parker Bidder, builder of London's Victoria docks in the nineteenth century, could figure problems like "How many times does 15,228 go into the cube of 36" in four seconds. Bidder's brother memorized the entire Bible and could remember every date he ever read. George Bidder's eldest son, George Bidder Jr., was able to multiply a fifteen-digit number by another fifteen-digit number mentally in less than a minute.

Oscar Verhaeghe of Uccle, Belgium, can multiply four-digit numbers by two-digit numbers in fifteen seconds without pencil and paper. Verhaeghe can give square roots, cube enormous numbers, and square large sums in less than half a minute. Once, under test conditions, he calculated the square of 888,888,888,888,888 in forty seconds (the answer is 790,123,426,790,121,876,543,209,876,544). Except for his mathematical ability, Verhaeghe, now well on in years, has the mental capacity of a child.

The Babylonians developed a series of advanced quadratic equations centuries before the birth of Christ.

When one adds up the number of letters in the names of the playing cards—ace (3), two (3), three (5), four (4), five (4), six (3), seven (5), eight (5), nine (4), ten (3), jack (4), queen (5), king (4)—the total comes to 52, the precise number of cards in a deck.

According to modern theories of higher mathematics:

If a person approached the speed of light he would shrink to a tiny size.

If a person surpassed the speed of light he would start moving backward in time.

The shortest distance between two points is a curve, not a line.

Parallel lines eventually meet.

Time is a curve.

Space is, paradoxically, at the same time both infinite and bounded.

There is no such thing as a straight line in the universe.

The faster an object moves in space the heavier it becomes—but at the same time, the smaller it becomes as well.

If one started counting the moment he or she was born and continued counting without stopping until he or she reached the age of sixty-five, that person still would not have counted to a billion.

If at the birth of Christ someone began to spend a dollar every second and continued spending up to the present time, that person would have spent less than $62 billion.

If you are thirty-five years old you have lived approximately 12,800 days. If you are fifty you have lived 18,300 days. If sixty, 21,900 days; if seventy-five, 27,400.

If a person places a single coin on the first square of a chessboard, then places twice this number, or two coins, on the second square, twice this number again, or four coins, on the third, and so on until all sixty-four squares are covered, exactly 18,446,744,973,709,551,661 coins will be required to do the job—more than have been minted in the world since the beginning of recorded civilization.

If one counted twenty-four hours a day, it would take 31,688 years to count to a trillion. If a trillion dollar bills were stacked one on top of the other the stack would be twice as high as Mount Everest. A trillion dollar bills laid end to end would circle the world 3,882 times.

Medicine

Twenty minutes before the pain of a migraine headache begins, many sufferers experience a phenomenon called the aura. During this time the sufferer may see intense colors, flashing lights, even monsters and apparitions. Lewis Carroll, a migraine victim most of his life, is supposed to have taken some of his characters for *Alice in Wonderland* from the apparitions he saw before attacks.

In 1374 at Aix-la-Chapelle during the siege of the Black Death, a thousand men, women, and children lost all control, joined hands, and danced in the streets, shrieking and maiming each other until they all died of wounds or fatigue.

According to the American Society for the Study of Headaches 80 percent of migraine sufferers are women.

English townspeople fleeing to the country to escape the Plague

The Black Plague destroyed half the population of Europe in the fourteenth century.

The mortality rate for infectious diseases is lowest between the ages of five and fifteen. After twenty-five the body is much more susceptible to disease.

There is a disease called ichthyosis that turns the skin scaly like a fish.

Humans are susceptible to a disease called the "laughing sickness." People stricken with this disease literally laugh themselves to death. The disease is known in only one place in the world, among the Kuru tribe of New Guinea.

According to the National Health Foundation, after suffering a cold one should wait at least six days before kissing someone.

Dr. John Cohausen wrote a book in 1743 "proving" that one could live to be 115 years old by inhaling the breath of little girls. In his book, *Hermippus Redivivus,* Dr. Cohausen gave the following prescription: take 1 pound of gum olibani, 2 ounces of styrae, myrrh, and several other herbs, mix, burn, and inhale while at the same time imbibing the exhalations of the nearest little girl.

The primary source of physical discomfort among Americans is back pain.

People recovering from a cold may find rubbing noses less risky than kissing. Sculpture by Gustav Vigeland in the Vigeland Museum, Oslo.

Wyoming has fewer than 1,000 cases of cancer each year. New York State has the highest incidence, with more than 70,000 cancer victims each year.

Statistics indicate that girls who have intercourse early in life, particularly before the age of sixteen, are twice as likely to develop cancer of the cervix as those who do not begin having intercourse until they are in their twenties.

According to the American Heart Association, although people on a low-saturated-fat diet have a 20 percent lower death rate from heart disease than people on a normal diet, they have a 30 percent higher death rate from cancer.

According to scientists from Harvard, Western Reserve, and New Mexico universities, the death rate from coronary heart disease is 28 percent lower among males who live above 7,000 feet than it is among those who live at altitudes between 3,000 and 4,000 feet.

Women who work have fewer heart problems than men who work. Women in general have remarkably fewer heart attacks than men.

One out of every four Americans will get cancer. Cancer causes one death in the United States every 90 seconds.

The average waiting time in a doctor's office, the American Medical Association reports, is twenty minutes. If the doctor is a family physician, the average waiting time can be as long as half an hour. Waiting time for a psychiatrist, however, is usually less than five minutes.

In ancient China doctors were paid when their patients were kept well, not when they were sick. Believing that it was the doctor's job to prevent disease, Chinese doctors often paid the patient if the patient lost his health. Further, if a patient died, a special lantern was hung outside the doctor's house. At each death another lantern was added. Too many of these lanterns were certain to ensure a slow trade.

More than half a million Americans died during the influenza epidemic of 1918.

According to Planned Parenthood, the number of legal abortions in the United States has increased by 20 percent each year since 1974. Legal abortions, says the organization, are now the second most common surgical operation in the United States, second only to tonsillectomies.

The jaws of African fire ants are used as sutures for wounds in Kenya, Uganda, and parts of South Africa. After an operation is performed, an ant is allowed to bite into the two flaps of skin along the line of the incision. The ant's body is then twisted off, leaving the head with its mandibles locked into the skin like a stitch. A number of these miniature "stitches" are placed along a wound. During the healing process, they closely resemble modern surgical stitching.

Pirates believed that piercing the ears and wearing an earring improved eyesight. This idea, scoffed at for centuries, has been reevaluated in light of acupuncture theory. The point on the lobe where the ear was pierced corresponds to the auricular acupuncture point controlling the eyes.

Pirate's earring may have improved his eyesight. Illustration by Howard Pyle from *The Book of Pirates*.

Minerals & Precious Metals

Most precious gems are actually colorless. Their color comes from impurities in the stone that act as pigmenting agents.

Sterling silver is not pure silver. Because pure silver is too soft to be used in most tableware it is mixed with copper in the proportion of 92.5 percent silver to 7.5 percent copper.

Twenty-four-karat gold is not pure gold; there is a small amount of copper in it. Absolutely pure gold is so soft that it can be molded with the hands.

The best diamonds are colored blue-white.

Some of the world's most celebrated diamonds, including the Hope (bottom row, 2nd from right) and the Kohinoor (2nd row from bottom, far right)

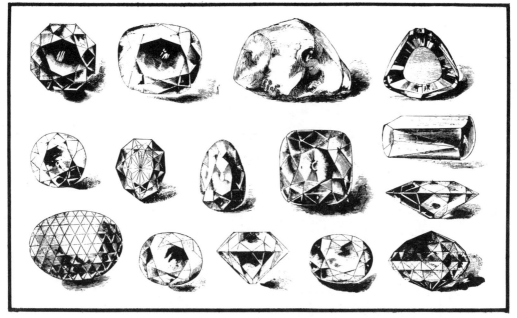

The ruby, sapphire, and emerald are not specific minerals. A ruby is the red, a sapphire the blue, variety of corundum. An emerald is the green, an aquamarine the blue, variety of beryl.

The term "magnetism" is derived from the region of Magnesia in Asia Minor, where a black mineral known as the lodestone is mined. Because of its magnetic properties, the lodestone was used by ancient seamen to navigate their ships, as a compass is used today.

Crystals grow by reproducing themselves. They come nearest to being "alive" of all members of the mineral kingdom.

Money

The first coin minted in the United States was a silver dollar. It was issued on October 15, 1794.

On March 16, 1970, a bidder at Sotheby & Company in London paid $20,000 for one glass paperweight.

During the American revolution, inflation was so great that the price of corn rose 10,000 percent, the price of wheat 14,000 percent, the price of flour 15,000 percent, and the price of beef 33,000 percent.

A quarter has 119 grooves on its circumference. A dime has one less.

Assuming that each fold neatly overlaps its opposite side, a dollar bill can be folded only six times—seven if put into a vise. (Try it.)

In 1915 the average annual family income in the United States was $687 a year.

In 1975 a birdhouse costing $10,000 was built in Quebec by the city fathers.

As of 1976 there was $77 billion worth of paper currency in circulation in the United States.

In 1060 a coin was minted in England shaped like a clover. The user could break off any of the four leaves and use them as separate pieces of currency.

During the early boom days of the Gold Rush in San Francisco a glass of whiskey could cost as much as $7.

Gold mine in California, 1854

Until the twentieth century dogs' teeth were used as money by Solomon Island natives.

In 1973 the United States Customs Service in New York City collected more than $1.3 billion in import duties.

According to the Nielson Clearing House in Clinton, Iowa, so many advertiser and manufacturer coupons are redeemed in America each year that if their value were averaged out per capita, every person in the United States would receive $1.25 in cash—this though the average coupon is worth only 14 cents.

More than a million dollars belonging to Adolf Hitler and other prominent Nazis is still unclaimed in American banks. The money was deposited several years before America entered World War II and no one knows what to do with it today.

One-fourth of the world's population lives on less than $200 a year. Ninety million people survive on less than $75 a year.

During the early 1920's, at the height of the inflation in the German Weimar Republic, one American dollar was equal to 4 trillion German marks.

In 1965, a collection of eight bottles of Château Lafite Rothschild was sold at auction for $2,200.

The percentage of income tax paid by the average American family has more than doubled since 1953. In 1953 the average family paid 11 percent of its income out in taxes. In 1976 it paid 23 percent.

The amount of play money printed each year for use in the Parker Brothers game *Monopoly* totals more than the amount of real currency issued annually by the United States Government. As of 1974, according to Parker Brothers, almost 70 million *Monopoly* sets had been sold throughout the world.

It costs more to buy a new car today in the United States than it cost Christopher Columbus to equip and undertake three voyages to and from the New World.

Until the nineteenth century, solid blocks of tea were used as money in Siberia.

America once issued a 5-cent bill.

In 1776 a man who made $4,000 a year was considered wealthy.

As of 1976 there were approximately 375 ten-thousand-dollar bills in circulation in the United States.

There are six coins currently minted by the United States Treasury: the silver dollar, the 50-cent piece, the quarter, the dime, the nickel, and the penny. The faces on all these coins look to the left with one exception. Which one? The penny.

The Yap islanders in the South Pacific use 18-foot-high stone rings as money. The stones sometimes weigh as much as 15 tons, which means that when someone is paid in such currency, he goes to where the money is, not vice-versa.

Movies & Movie Stars

The cowboy movie star Tom Mix drove a Rolls-Royce that had a pair of antlers as a radiator cap. Mix once ordered tires for his limousine with his initials printed in relief. At that time Hollywood was connected by a network of dirt roads; whenever Mix drove along one of these roads he would leave a long trail of "TM"'s imprinted in the dust.

Grace Kelly was the first motion-picture actress to appear on a postage stamp. In April, 1956, she was featured with her husband, Prince Rainier III of Monaco, on a stamp that commemorated their wedding.

Alfred Hitchcock directed the first talking film ever made in England. It was called *Blackmail* and was made in 1931.

In 1939, Hollywood film companies produced an average of two motion pictures every day.

The figure of King Kong seen in the original movie of the same name was actually a model 18 inches high.

Scene from original
movie version
of *King Kong*, 1937

Vivien Leigh as Scarlett O'Hara and Leslie Howard as Ashley Wilkes in a scene from *Gone with the Wind*

During the casting of the film *Gone with the Wind,* more than 1,400 candidates were interviewed for the part of Scarlett O'Hara, and more than $92,000 was spent in the search.

The film *Quo Vadis* used 30,000 extras (and 63 lions).

Museums & Libraries

Wonalancet, New Hampshire, boasts the world's only Antarctic dog museum, the Byrd Antarctic Dog Memorial Museum.

The work of an artist cannot be exhibited in the Louvre until he has been dead for at least sixty years. The only exception ever made to this rule was Georges Braque.

James Smithson, English scientist and founder of the Smithsonian Institution, never once set foot in America. The Institution was established in 1846 with funds from his estate which he left for "the increase and diffusion of knowledge among men."

The Library of Congress has 327 miles of bookshelves.

Old Lyme, Connecticut has the world's only museum dedicated to nuts. The world's largest nutcracker, 8 feet long, hangs outside on a tree.

The Smithsonian Institution has over 30 million fossils in its paleontology collection and more than 24 million insect specimens.

Music & Musicians

Mozart wrote the opera *Don Giovanni* at one sitting. It was played without rehearsal the day after it was written.

Haydn could write music only on clean white paper. Mozart composed while playing billiards. Christoph Gluck would write only when seated in the middle of a field. Rossini composed most of his music when he was drunk. Wagner found it easiest to compose when he was dressed up in historical costumes. Haydn believed he could not compose well unless he was wearing a ring given to him by Frederick the Great.

Richard Wagner

The famous Russian composer Alexander Borodin was a professor of chemistry at the Academy of Medicine in St. Petersburg. Borodin always referred to himself as a "musical amateur."

The song most frequently sung in the western world is "Happy Birthday to You." The song was written in 1936 by Mildred and Patty Hill, and their estate still collects royalties on it.

Fifty-three operas have been written about Faust.

The oboe is considered the most difficult of all woodwind instruments to play correctly.

Wooden clarinets are always made of wood from the granadilla tree.

Felix Mendelssohn wrote his most famous overture, *A Midsummer Night's Dream,* when he was seventeen.

Lewis H. Dedner, composer of the music to "O Little Town of Bethlehem," claimed that the hymn's melody came to him in a dream on Christmas Eve. Charles Wesley, author of "Hark, the Herald Angels Sing" (written in 1730), wrote a total of 6,000 hymns. He was inspired to write "Hark" while listening to the pealing of bells as he walked to church one Christmas morning.

Beethoven was totally deaf when he composed his Ninth Symphony.

Ludwig van Beethoven

Ignace Paderewski, one of the greatest concert pianists of all time, was also premier of Poland.

Cello and saxophone players, as of 1975, could join the Marine Corps and play in the band without taking basic training.

Verdi wrote the opera *Aida* at the request of the khedive of Egypt to commemorate the opening of the Suez Canal.

"The Washington Post March" by John Philip Sousa was named after a newspaper, the Washington *Post*.

Franz Liszt was Richard Wagner's father-in-law. Arturo Toscanini was Vladimir Horowitz's father-in-law.

Franz Liszt

More than 100 descendants of Johann Sebastian Bach have been cathedral organists.

The oldest piano still in existence was built in 1720.

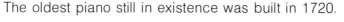

Piano built by Bartolomeo Cristofori in Florence, 1720

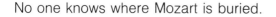

No one knows where Mozart is buried.

The cello's real name is the violoncello. The full name of the piano is the pianoforte.

Wolfgang Amadeus Mozart

The Greek national anthem has 158 verses.

Dr. Friederich Mesmer, Austrian physician and the inventor of mesmerism, a forerunner of hypnosis, introduced the harmonica to France.

Franz Schubert's masterpiece, his Sixth Symphony, was turned down by the Paris Symphony Orchestra. The London Philharmonic laughed at it, and its conductor withdrew it from rehearsal. The piece was not played publicly until thirty years after it was written.

Names: People, Places, & Things

What have the following towns in common: Dayton, Atlanta, Cleveland, Philadelphia, Jacksonville, Norfolk, Bangor, Hartford, New Haven, Phoenix, Stamford, Urbana, and Newark? They are all towns in New York State.

The initials BVD, which have come to stand for men's underwear in general, stand for the names of the three men who originally manufactured BVDs—Bradley, Voorhies, and Day.

The town of Modesto, California, was named in honor of its founders, who were too "modest" to name it after themselves. The town of Tarzana, California, is named for the fictional character Tarzan, having been the home for many years of Edgar Rice Burroughs, creator of the Tarzan saga.

The official name of India is not India. It is Bharat.

The first letter of every continent's name is the same as the last: AmericA, AntarcticA, EuropE, AsiA, AustraliA, AfricA.

Muhammad is the most common name in the world.

The word "Nazi" was actually an abbreviation. The party's full name was the *Nazionalsozialistische Deutsche Arbeiterpartei.*

Cotton Mather, famous American clergyman, had an odd first name. His father had an even odder one: Increase.

Maine is the only state in the United States whose name has one syllable.

Battleships are always named after states, submarines after fish, cruisers after cities, and destroyers after naval heroes.

Until 1796, there was a state in the United States called Franklin. Today it is known as Tennessee.

There were 2,282 people named Smith in the 1975 Manhattan telephone directory.

Their real names:
    Hieronymus Bosch—Hieronymus van Aken
    Sandro Botticelli—Alessandro di Mariano dei Filipepi
    Anthony Burgess—John Wilson
    El Cid—Rodrigo Díaz de Bivar
    Joseph Conrad—Teodor Korzeniowski
    Le Corbusier—Charles Edouard Jeanneret
    Marie Corelli—Mary Mackay
    Donatello—Donato di Niccolò di Betto Bardi
    George Eliot—Mary Ann Evans
    Anatole France—Jacques Thibault
    Maxim Gorky—Alexey Peshkov
    Lenin—Vladimir Ulyanov
    "Baby Face" Nelson—Lester Gillis
    George Orwell—Eric Blair
    Ellery Queen—Frederic Dunnay and Manfred B. Lee
    George Sand—Amandine Aurore Lucie Dupin, Baronne Dudevant
    "Dutch" Schultz—Arthur Flegenheimer
    Josef Stalin—Josef Dzhugashvili
    Emanuel Swedenborg—Emanuel Swedberg
    Tintoretto—Jacopo Robusti
    Jules Verne—L. M. Olehewitz
    Voltaire—François Marie Arouet

The blazer jacket is named for a British ship, H.M.S. *Blazer*. The ship's captain insisted that his crew always wear blue jackets with metal buttons, even for casual duty.

Benito Mussolini was named after a Mexican revolutionary and liberal statesman, Benito Juárez.

Benito Mussolini

The name "pumpernickel" was coined by Napoleon's troops during the Napoleonic Wars. His men complained that although they were often poorly fed, there was always bread for Napoleon's favorite horse, Nicoll. Thus the word "pumpernickel" was coined—*pain* (bread) *pour* (for) Nicoll.

The following are all names of men who have played major-league baseball:

Eli Grba, Malachi Kittredge, Tacks Neuer, Prince Oana, Orval Overall, Ty Pickup, Squiz Pillon, Shadow Pyle, Ossie Schreckengost, Tony Suck, Clay Touchstone, Coot Veal, Yats Wuestling, Ad Yale.

When the planet Uranus was discovered by Sir William Herschel in 1781 it was named "Georgium Sidium" in honor of King George III of England. For many years the planet was known as the "Georgian." Not until 1850 was it christened

Uranus in accordance with the tradition of naming planets for Roman gods.

Named after:

Bloomers were the brainstorm of Amelia Bloomer, who caused a scandal by wearing trousers that exposed two inches of her ankles.

The *braille* reading system is named for Louis Braille. Blinded in an accident at age three, Braille became one of the most brilliant prodigies of his time and invented his famous reading method while still in his twenties.

The *chesterfield* settee is named after a nineteenth-century Earl of Chesterfield.

The *derrick* is named after Thomas Derrick, a seventeenth-century English executioner-hangman whose association with the gallows gave his name to the crane.

The *doily* is named after a Mr. Doiley, a seventeenth-century linendraper in London.

The *guillotine* is named after Dr. Joseph Guillotin. Guillotin did not invent the deadly mechanism—it had been in

Above: Amelia Bloomer wearing the garment she attempted to popularize
Left: Execution by guillotine during the French revolution

use for centuries before his time—but suggested it in the eighteenth century as a humane method of execution.

The *Norfolk jacket* is named for a nineteenth-century Duke of Norfolk.

The *Oscar* film trophy is named after Oscar Pierce, a wealthy Texas farmer. Before the trophy had any name at all, Pierce's niece, then serving as librarian for the

Academy of Motion Picture Arts and Sciences, commented that the statue reminded her of her Uncle Oscar. A newspaper columnist overheard the chance remark and subsequently wrote that "employees have affectionately dubbed their famous statuette 'Oscar.' " The name stuck.

The *peach Melba* is named after Dame Nellie Melba, an Australian operatic soprano, for whom the dish was first created.

The *saxophone* is named after Antoine Sax. Born in Belgium, Sax invented a number of unusual-sounding brass instruments, all of which he named after himself. Besides the saxophone he created the saxhorn and the saxotromba.

The *silhouette* is named after Etienne de Silhouette, a French author and statesman who reputedly was highly skilled at the art of cutting profiles out of paper.

The *tam o' shanter* is named for the hero of Robert Burns's poem of the same name.

Wellington boots were the invention of Arthur Wellesley, first Duke of Wellington.

Natural Phenomena

When the volcano Krakatoa erupted in the Dutch East Indies in 1883, the sound was heard in Bangkok, 3,000 miles away. At Batavia, 100 miles away, the sky was so darkened that people had to light their lamps during the day. The fine particles ejected by the blast covered almost every part of the world, and for the next two years a thin haze of these particles could be seen in the sky each night as far away as London.

There are more than 50,000 earthquakes throughout the world every year.

More than 71 million gallons of water pass over Victoria Falls in Africa every minute.

Venezuela's Angel Falls are a mile high.

One can see the stars during the day from the bottom of a well.

The Niagara Falls have eroded their way 10 miles upstream since they were first formed some 10,000 years ago. The tremendous amount of water tends to eat through its limestone base relatively rapidly, and if erosion continues at its present rate, geologists estimate that the falls will disappear completely in 22,000 years.

Still majestic, Niagara Falls may be slowly disappearing.

Old Faithful in Yellowstone National Park, Wyoming, is *not* the highest natural geyser in the United States. Its neighbor, the Beehive Geyser, spouts well over 200 feet of water, compared with Old Faithful's 160. The Beehive, however, performs its majestic ejections at infrequent and unpredictable intervals.

People

Thomas Edison was deaf from the time he was twelve years old. The malady was caused while Edison was trying to board a train at Frazer Station, Michigan. A conductor took hold of his ears to help pull him aboard. "I felt something snap inside my head," Edison later said. "My deafness

Thomas Edison's impaired hearing did not impede his brilliance as an inventor.

started from that time and has progressed ever since." Edison never went to school—his formal education consisted of three months' attendance at a public school in Port Huron, Michigan.

Faust, the protagonist of works by Christopher Marlowe, Goethe, and dozens of other writers, was an actual person. Johann Faust was a sixteenth-century doctor of theology at the University of Wittenberg in Germany. Many stories were told about him during his lifetime, including one in which he sold his soul to the devil in exchange for eternal youth and wisdom. The tale captured the imagination of authors for centuries afterward.

Napoleon had conquered Italy by the time he was twenty-six.

Arthur Conan Doyle, author of the Sherlock Holmes stories, was an ophthalmologist by profession.

Christopher Columbus had blond hair.

Karl Marx once served as a reporter on the New York *Herald Tribune* (the paper was then known as the New York *Tribune*). In 1848 he worked in the London office of the *Tribune,* and his boss, the managing editor, was Richard Henry Dana, who himself became world-famous as author of *Two Years Before the Mast.*

Sir Christopher Wren, designer of St. Paul's Cathedral in London, was not an architect. He was a mathematician and an astronomer. Wren was in fact a great astronomer, having developed a method for computing eclipses and another for measuring the rings of Saturn.

The longest biographical entry in the 1975 edition of *Who's Who* is that of Buckminster Fuller, the well-known American architect, engineer, and designer.

Casanova, the greatest adventurer and lover of his time, ended his life as a librarian. From 1785 to 1798 he lived in Bohemia, semiretired, working as librarian for Count von Waldstein in the Château de Dux. He died quietly at the job.

Giovanni Jacopo Casanova

Lord Byron had four pet geese that he brought everywhere with him, even to social gatherings. Byron, though considered one of the most dashing and attractive men of his time, was fat and had a club foot.

Romantic portrait of George Gordon, Lord Byron, by Vincenzo Camuccini

Julius Caesar, Alexander the Great, and Dostoyevsky were all epileptics.

Alexandre Dumas *père* was one-quarter black.

There is absolutely no documented proof that Betsy Ross designed the American flag.

Attila the Hun was a dwarf. Pepin the Short, Aesop, Gregory of Tours, Charles III of Naples, and the Pasha Hussain were all less than 3½ feet tall.

Rudyard Kipling would only write when he had black ink in his pen. Beethoven poured ice water over his head when he sat down to create music, believing it stimulated his brain. Dickens wrote (and slept) facing north, aligning himself with the poles of the earth. Rossini covered himself with blankets when he composed. Proust worked in bed, and only in a soundproof room.

In 1898 P. T. Barnum's side show included a man who looked like a Skye terrier; a woman with a goatee; a woman with scaly alligatorlike skin; a blue man (he had permanently dyed himself by accident with silver nitrate); the most tattooed woman in the world (she claimed to have been stabbed by the tattooer's needle 100 million times); a Ubangi with saucers in both lips; an "India-rubber man" who could pull the skin several inches off his cheeks; a woman whom no one could make laugh (her facial muscles were paralyzed); a "hardheaded man" (people could break blocks of granite over his skull. A doctor once examined him and found his skull to be 2 inches thick); an ossified man (his flesh had completely hardened and crystallized before he died); a "living skeleton" (6 feet tall and 70 pounds); a "gorilla girl" (billed as the ugliest woman in the world); and "What Is It," a congenital idiot so misshapen and retarded that some people believed him to be an unknown species of monkey.

One of Napoleon's drinking cups was made from the skull of the famous Italian adventurer Cagliostro.

Henry Wadsworth Longfellow, who made John and Priscilla Alden famous in his poem "The Courtship of Miles Standish," was related to both these actual historical personages.

Tom Fuller, a slave brought to America when he was fourteen years old, could tell the exact number of seconds in any given length of time. Once, when asked to give the precise number of seconds in seventy years, he obliged in less than one and a half minutes. Yet Fuller could neither read nor write.

Lafayette was a major general in the United States at the age of nineteen. Lafayette's whole name takes up an entire line on a page: Marie Joseph Paul Yves Roch Gilbert du Motier, Marquis de Lafayette.

Lafayette conferring with George Washington at Mount Vernon, detail of a painting by Horace K. Turner after Thomas Rossiter

An eighteenth-century German named Matthew Birchinger, known as "the little man of Nuremberg," played four musical instruments including the bagpipes, was an expert calligrapher, and was the most famous stage magician of his

The "little man of Nuremberg"

day. He performed tricks with the cup and balls that have never been explained. Yet Birchinger had no hands, legs, or thighs, and was less than 29 inches tall.

There is absolutely no evidence that Adolf Hitler was a paperhanger.

The African country of Rhodesia is named after an English entrepreneur, Cecil Rhodes. Rhodes, prime minister of Cape Colony in South Africa in the late nineteenth century and creator of the South Africa diamond syndicate, at one time controlled 90 percent of the world's supply of diamonds. When he died, in 1902, his will stipulated that a great part of his fortune was to be used for the establishment of a foundation for the furtherance of higher education, which today grants the Rhodes Scholarship.

Nobody knows where the body of Voltaire is. It was stolen from its tomb in the nineteenth century and has never been recovered. The theft was discovered in 1864, when the tomb was opened and found empty.

The Mongol conqueror Timur the Lame (1336–1405), whom Christopher Marlowe called Tamburlaine, played polo with the skulls of those he had killed in battle. Timur left records of his victories by erecting 30-foot-high pyramids made of the severed heads of his victims.

There are a number of Americans who are related to Napoleon Bonaparte. Napoleon's youngest brother, Jerome, married an American.

Napoleon in His Study,
by Jacques Louis David

The famous nineteenth-century bullfighter Lagartijo (born Rafael Molina) killed 4,867 bulls.

The Graham cracker was named after Sylvester Graham (1794–1851). A New England minister, Graham not only invented the cracker but also published a journal in Boston that took a rabid stand against tea, coffee, feather beds, and women's corsets.

Alexandre Gustave Eiffel, the man who designed the Eiffel Tower, also designed the inner structure of the Statue of Liberty in New York Harbor.

James A. Garfield

President James Garfield could write Latin with one hand and Greek with the other—simultaneously! Leonardo da Vinci could draw with one hand and write with the other, also simultaneously.

The Second Marquess of Ripon, a well-known British sportsman, killed a total of 556,000 gamebirds in his life. The Marquess dropped dead on a grouse hunt in 1923, after having bagged 52 birds that morning.

Irénée Du Pont, onetime president of E. I. Du Pont de Nemours and Company, kept pet iguanas on his estate in Cuba. Mr. Du Pont spent many hours training these pets and succeeded in teaching them to stand at attention and to come when called.

Pierre Beaumarchais, one of the leading French dramatists of the eighteenth century, invented a device called the escapement, without which modern wristwatches would have been impossible. Beaumarchais was one of the most important Frenchmen to fight on the side of the colonies in the American revolution, was a secret agent for Louis XVI and gave harp lessons to the King's daughter, instituted in France the practice of paying playwrights royalties for their performed works, spent several years in jail for bank fraud and treason and pleaded his own case in court several times, edited the works of Voltaire, and wrote the operas *The Barber of Seville* and *The Marriage of Figaro*.

David Kennison, born in 1736, lived to 115 and was the longest-surviving participant in the Boston Tea Party. He served in both the American revolution and the War of 1812. He served in the latter at the age of seventy-six, and had his hand shot off at Sackett's Harbor. Several years later, his skull was fractured when a tree fell on his head, and several years after that, while he was training for a militia drill, a premature explosion from a cannon shattered both his legs. When he recovered from the injury, his legs became covered with sores that never healed, and he was stricken with rheumatism. Some time later, his face was mutilated when he was kicked by a horse. He finally died a quiet death in Illinois in 1851.

After Sir Isaac Newton died, a sealed trunk was found among his belongings containing nearly 100,000 pages he had written on the subjects of alchemy, astrology, and the occult.

Sir Richard Burton (1821–1890), the English explorer and the first westerner ever to enter the sacred Moslem city of

Mecca, spoke twenty languages, almost discovered the source of the Nile, fought Indians with Kit Carson, was a close friend of Brigham Young, was one of the first white men to sail down the Amazon, and wrote the first western translation of *The Arabian Nights*.

Sir Richard Burton in 1857

Charles Carroll, one of the signers of the Declaration of Independence, lived long enough to help lay the cornerstone of the Baltimore & Ohio Railroad in 1828. Carroll, the longest-lived of all the signers, died in 1832 at the age of ninety-five.

When the circus dwarf Lavinia Bump married the circus dwarf Tom Thumb, more than 2,000 guests attended their

Wedding portrait of
Mr. and Mrs. Tom Thumb

wedding, including President and Mrs. Abraham Lincoln and the entire United States Cabinet. The famous ceremony was dubbed "The Fairy Wedding."

Charles Lindbergh was instrumental in the development of a method for preserving human tissue outside the body. He coauthored a book on the subject, *The Culture of Organs,* with the French scientist Alexis Carrel. Lindbergh was also among the first to perfect a mechanical heart, a pumping apparatus that supplied blood to organs to keep them alive outside the body.

Both Josef Stalin and Kaiser Wilhelm had crippled left arms. Stalin, despite his popular image, was not a pipe smoker. He used the pipe only for effect at conferences and public appearances. In private he chain-smoked cigarettes.

When he was a child, Blaise Pascal once locked himself in his room for several days and would not allow anyone to enter. When he emerged, he had figured out all of Euclid's geometrical propositions totally on his own.

Edgar Allan Poe and James Abbott McNeill Whistler both went to West Point.

The English poet Thomas Chatterton died at seventeen. Mozart died at thirty-six, Raphael died at thirty-seven, Aubrey Beardsley died at twenty-six, and the painter Masaccio died at twenty-seven.

The Death of Chatterton, by H. Wallis

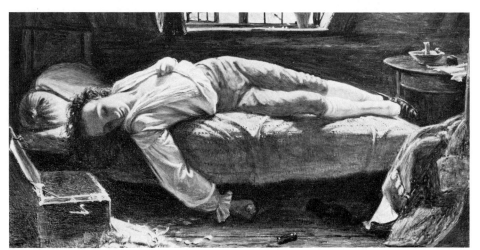

The famous Swedish astronomer Tycho Brahe had a nose made of gold. It was a replacement for his own, which he lost in a duel with a Danish nobleman in 1566.

Geoffry Hudson, a famous dwarf at the seventeenth-century court of Charles II of England, stood 3 feet high and enjoyed entertaining the king by popping out of large pastries. Hudson once fought a duel against a full-sized man for a full-sized woman and won.

Edward Hyde, Viscount Cornbury, colonial governor of New York and New Jersey from 1702 to 1708, was a professed transvestite. He commonly robed himself in women's outfits, rouged and powdered his face, and promenaded through the town in drag. He was once arrested on a morals charge. For his official portrait Viscount Cornbury posed in a low-cut evening gown holding a fan and wearing a sprig of lace in his hair. He was fired in 1708—not for his outrageous behavior, but for taking bribes.

Physics

An ice cube in a glass of water will not raise the water level when it melts. The amount of space it displaces as a cube is equal to the amount it takes up when liquefied.

All snow crystals are hexagonal.

No one can drown in the Dead Sea. It is 25 percent salt, which makes the water very heavy. This property makes a body extremely buoyant on the Dead Sea, so that it is almost impossible to remain submerged.

A ball of glass will bounce higher than a ball made of rubber. A ball of solid steel will bounce higher than one made entirely of glass.

In one second 6,242,000,000,000,000,000 electrons pass any given point in an electrical current.

Dry ice does not melt. It evaporates.

When glass breaks the cracks move faster than 3,000 miles per hour. To photograph the event a camera must shoot at a millionth of a second.

Where there is fire there is not always smoke. Smoke simply means that a fire is not burning properly and that bits of un-burned materials are escaping. A perfectly clean fire pro-duces almost no smoke.

If hot water is suddenly poured into a glass the glass is more apt to break if it is thick than if it is thin. This is why test tubes are made of thin glass.

A bubble is round because the air within it presses equally against all its parts, thus causing all surfaces to be equidis-tant from its center.

Nothing can be burned again that has already been burned once.

The color black absorbs heat. White reflects it.

A whip makes a cracking sound because its tip moves faster than the speed of sound (760 miles per hour).

Gasoline has no specific freezing point—it freezes at any temperature between -180° and -240° F (-118° to -151° C). When it does freeze it never solidifies totally, but resembles gum or wax.

An egg will float if placed in water to which sugar has been added.

It takes as much heat to turn one ounce of snow to water as it does to make an ounce of soup boil at room tem-perature.

Dirty snow melts faster than clean.

Granite conducts sound ten times faster than air.

Water has a greater molecular density in liquid form than as a solid. This is why ice floats.

If a glass of water were magnified to the size of the earth, the molecules comprising it would be about as big as a large orange.

Hot water weighs more than cold.

Predictions

Roger Bacon, a thirteenth-century Franciscan monk, predicted the following things in his *Communia Mathematica:*

High-speed sea travel. "It is possible to make machines of navigation," wrote the erudite monk, "which need no man to navigate them, so that very large seagoing ships may go along with one man to steer, and at a greater speed than if they were full of men working them."

The automobile. "Cars could be made which move at inestimable speed without animals to draw them as if they were the chariots in which men fought of old."

The airplane. "Flying machines can be built so that a man sitting in the middle of the machine may turn an instrument by which wings artificially made will beat the air, like a bird flying."

First airplane flight, December 17, 1903. Pilot was Orville Wright.

The microscope and telescope. "Instruments can be designed so that enormous things will appear very small, and contrariwise . . ."

Gunpowder and bombs. "Sounds like thunder can be made in the air but more terrifying than those which occur in nature; for an appropriate material in moderate quantity, as big as a man's thumb, makes a horrible noise and shows a violent flash; and this can be done in many ways by which a whole town or army may be destroyed."

Presidents

Franklin D. Roosevelt's birthday is a legal holiday in the Virgin Islands.

The teddy bear was named for Theodore Roosevelt. When presented with a koala from Australia, Roosevelt, whose fondness for animals was well known, so praised the creature that a copy of it was made for children. Called the "teddy bear" in the President's honor, the toy soon caught on and became a standard item on every child's shelf.

Grover Cleveland is the only United States president to have been married in the White House.

President and
Mrs. Grover Cleveland

James Madison, 5 feet, 4 inches tall, was the shortest president of the United States. Abraham Lincoln was the tallest at 6 feet, 4 inches.

James Madison

During World War I, Woodrow Wilson's wife grazed sheep on the front lawn of the White House.

President Taft weighed 352 pounds.

Thomas Jefferson, John Adams, and James Monroe all died on July 4th. Jefferson and Adams died at practically the same minute of the same day.

Martin Van Buren, eighth president of the United States, was the first to be born a citizen of the United States. He was born in 1782, six years after the signing of the Constitution.

Martin Van Buren

In 1824, Andrew Jackson received more popular votes than John Adams, yet lost the election. The vote was so close that neither candidate received a majority of the electoral votes. The decision then went to the House of Representatives, which elected Adams.

President Grover Cleveland was a draft dodger. He hired someone to enter the service in his place, for which he was ridiculed by his political opponent, James G. Blaine. It was soon discovered, however, that Blaine had done the same thing himself.

For his entire forty-seven years in government, Herbert Hoover turned over each of his Federal salary checks to charity. He had become independently wealthy before entering politics.

George Washington's face was badly scarred from smallpox.

Theodore Roosevelt became president at the age of forty-two. He was the youngest president ever to hold office.

Theodore Roosevelt

William Howard Taft is the only man ever to have been both chief justice and president of the United States.

In 1920 Socialist Eugene Debs received 920,000 votes for president of the United States. Yet he ran his entire campaign while in jail.

In 1976 President Gerald R. Ford sent out 40,000 Christmas cards.

Theodore Roosevelt was Eleanor Roosevelt's uncle.

President John Tyler had fifteen children.

At the inauguration of Abraham Lincoln in 1860 four future presidents were in attendance: Benjamin Harrison, Chester Alan Arthur, Rutherford B. Hayes, and James A. Garfield.

Zachary Taylor, twelfth president of the United States, did not vote until he was sixty-two. He did not even vote in his own election. Taylor, a professional soldier, lived in so many places during his life that he was unable to establish a legal residence until he retired.

Zachary Taylor

Gerald Ford was one of the members of the Warren Commission appointed to study the assassination of President John F. Kennedy.

Theodore Roosevelt's wife and mother both died on the same day.

James Buchanan was the only United States president never to marry. During his term in office, his niece Harriet Lane played the role of First Lady.

James Buchanan

George Washington left no direct descendants. Though his wife Martha had four children by a previous marriage, Washington never sired a child to continue his line.

Franklin D. Roosevelt, the most popular president ever to hold office in the United States, did not carry his home county of Dutchess, New York, in any of his four elections.

John F. Kennedy and Warren Harding were the only United States presidents to be survived by their fathers.

George Washington was *not* the first president of the United States. The first president was John Hanson, Maryland's representative at the Continental Congress. On November 5, 1781, Hanson was elected by the Constitutional Congress to the office of "President of the United States in Congress Assembled." He served for one year.

A man named David Rice Atchison was president of the United States for one day and didn't know it. According to a nineteenth-century law, if neither the president nor the vice-president was in office, the president pro tem of the Senate became chief executive. On March 4, 1849, President James Knox Polk's term had lapsed, and the newly elected Zachary Taylor could not yet be sworn in (it was a Sunday). So for one day Atchison was president. It was not until several months later that Atchison learned of this, as the law was then an obscure one. It has since been changed.

When Abraham Lincoln's funeral procession passed Ford's Theater, where Lincoln had been shot, one of the cornices fell off the building. When John Wilkes Booth leaped onto the stage after shooting the President, he tripped—on the American flag. A short time before his assassination Lincoln dreamed he was going to die, and he related his dream to the Senate.

On New Year's Day, 1907, Theodore Roosevelt shook hands with 8,513 people.

President Ulysses S. Grant was once arrested during his term of office. He was convicted of exceeding the Washington speed limit on his horse and was fined $20. President Franklin Pierce was arrested while in office for running over an old woman with his horse, but the case was dropped for insufficient evidence in 1853.

Ulysses S. Grant

Norfolk County, Massachusetts, is the birthplace of three United States presidents: John Adams, John Quincy Adams, and John F. Kennedy.

Robert Todd Lincoln, son of Abraham Lincoln, was present at the assassinations of three presidents: his father's, Presi-

dent Garfield's, and President McKinley's. After the last shooting, he refused ever to attend a state affair again.

Assassination of President James Garfield by Charles Guiteau, 1881

Psychology

There is no one who does not dream. Those who claim to have no dreams, laboratory tests have determined, simply forget their dreams more easily than others.

The color combination with the strongest visual impact is black on yellow. Next follow black on white, yellow on black, white on black, dark blue on white, and white on dark blue.

The Psychology Department of Dayton University reports that loud talk can be ten times more distracting than the sound of a jackhammer. Loud, incessant chatter can make a listener nervous and irritable, say the findings, and even start him on the road to insanity.

The short-term memory capacity for most people is between five and nine items or digits. This is one reason that phone numbers are seven digits long.

Studies done by the Psychology Department of DePauw University show that the principal reason people lie is to avoid punishment.

Man is the only animal that cries.

Men laugh longer, more loudly, and more often than women.

A list of odd phobias:
    Ailurophobia—fear of cats.
    Androphobia—fear of men.
    Apiphobia—fear of bees.
    Astraphobia—fear of storms.
    Aviophobia—fear of flying.
    Baccilophobia—fear of microbes.
    Ballistophobia—fear of bullets.
    Belonephobia—fear of needles and sharp, pointed objects.
    Clinophobia—fear of beds.
    Gephydrophobia—fear of crossing bridges.
    Iatrophobia—fear of doctors.
    Nyctophobia—fear of night.
    Ombrophobia—fear of rain.
    Otophobia—fear of opening one's eyes.
    Peccatophobia—fear of sinning.
    Sitophobia—fear of food.
    Taphephobia—fear of being buried alive.
    Thalassophobia—fear of the ocean.
    Trichophobia—fear of hair.
    Vestiphobia—fear of clothing.

The term "doing one's own thing" was coined by the Gestalt psychologist Fritz Perls. His "Gestalt Prayer" reads:

"I do my thing and you do your thing. I am not in this world to live up to your expectations and you are not in this world to live up to mine. You are you and I am I, and if by chance we find each other, it's beautiful. If not, it can't be helped."

Records

Babe Ruth, besides holding the world lifetime record for home runs up to the 1970's, holds the world record for strikeouts as well.

Babe Ruth in the 1920's

Harry Drake of Lakeside, California, competing in a foot-bow archery contest at Ivanpah Dry Lake, California, in October, 1970, shot an arrow that traveled 1 mile, 101 yards, and 21 inches. A foot bow is fired by lying on one's back, stringing the bow, and pushing out the wooden part of the bow with one's feet.

The record for traveling from New York to Los Angeles by motorcycle is 45 hours, 41 minutes. It was set in 1968 by Tibor Sarossy, riding a BMW Model R69S. Sarossy made four fuel stops, never slept, fainted twice, and averaged 58.7 miles per hour all the way across.

In June, 1963, in Britain, the British tennis player Michael Sangster served a ball that was clocked at 154 miles per hour. This is the fastest tennis serve ever recorded.

The best-selling nonfiction book of all time is Benjamin Spock's *Common Sense Book of Baby and Child Care.*

Religion

Throughout history, nearly all religions of the world have had a celebration that falls close to Christmas. In Judaism it is Hanukkah, the Festival of Lights. Pre-Christian Scandinavians enjoyed the Feast of the Frost King. In Rome there was the Saturnalia, in Egypt the midwinter festival in honor of the god Horus. The Druids had an annual mistletoe-cutting ceremony. Mithraists celebrated the feast of Sol Invictus, representing the victory of light over darkness. In Hinduism the feasts of Diwali and Taipongal are observed close to the Christmas season. Many other civilizations have similar festivals.

In the year 632, when the prophet Muhammad died, the Islamic empire comprised only an insignificant corner of Arabia. A little more than a hundred years later the Moslem religion had spread to Persia, Egypt, Syria, India, Central Asia, parts of northern Africa, and into southern Africa. In a century's time Islam had converted one-third of the world.

The toe of the metal statue of St. Peter in St. Peter's Cathedral, Rome, is worn down almost to a nub by the great number of pilgrims who have kissed it through the centuries.

The Roman Catholic population of the world is larger than that of all other Christian sects combined.

Hairs from the tail of a mule ridden by the crusader Peter the Hermit brought high prices as sacred relics throughout Europe in the fourteenth century.

Before the Chinese takeover of Tibet in 1952, 25 percent of the males in the country were Buddhist monks.

On the stone temples of Madura in southern India, there are more than 30 million carved images of gods and goddesses.

There have been 262 popes since Saint Peter.

Christianity has a billion followers. Islam is next in representation with half this number.

In the Greek monastery of Mount Athos *nothing* female is allowed. Men can enter but not women; roosters but no hens; horses but no mares; bulls but no cows. The border is patrolled by armed guards to ensure that nothing feminine passes the gates. It has been this way for more than 700 years.

Tibetan monks and Inca priests both practiced a brain operation called "trepanation," in which a small hole was drilled through the skull of a living person, right between the eyes. Its purpose was to stimulate the pineal gland and thereby induce a mystical state of consciousness. The operation is occasionally still practiced today.

Hugnes was archbishop of Reims in the tenth century when he was five years old. In the eleventh century Benedict IX was Pope at eleven years old.

The Puritans forbade the singing of Christmas carols.

Priests in ancient Egyptian temples plucked every hair from their bodies, including their eyebrows and eyelashes.

Ancient Egyptian priest, accompanied by a sacred scribe

Royalty

The Japanese emperor Hirohito is the 124th holder of his title. The same family has held the throne in Japan since the sixth century A.D. Hirohito has published several books on ichthyology (the study of fish) and is considered an expert on the subject.

Cleopatra was married to her own brother, Ptolemy.

Henry VIII's second wife, Anne Boleyn, had six fingers on one hand. She wore special gloves all her life to hide her deformity.

Louis XIV owned 413 beds.

Every queen named Jane has either been murdered, imprisoned, gone mad, died young, or been dethroned.

At the court of Louis XIV, prestige was measured by the height of the chair one was allowed to sit in. Only the King and Queen could sit in chairs with arms.

King George I of England couldn't speak a word of English. His native tongue was German (he came from Hanover, Germany); he communicated with his cabinet in French.

John Hancock signed his name in extra-large letters on the Declaration of Independence not out of self-esteem but so that King George III, notoriously poor-sighted, could read it without the aid of spectacles.

Louis XIV of France, the Sun King, had Jewish blood. It came to him through the bloodline of the Aragons of Spain, to whom he was related.

When Louis XIV and Marie-Thérèse were awakened in the morning, if the Queen sat up after the curtains had been parted and clapped her hands, the servants knew that the King had performed his royal duty the night before—intercourse with the Queen.

Berengaria, Queen of England and wife of Richard the Lionhearted, never set foot in England. She lived in Italy most of her life while her husband was off on adventures and crusades.

Jahangir, a seventeenth-century Indian Mughal ruler, had 5,000 women in his harem and 1,000 young boys. He also owned 12,000 elephants.

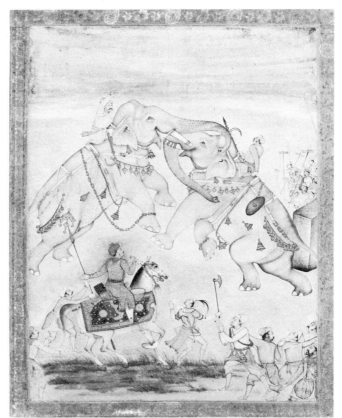

The Emperor Jahangir Viewing Fighting Elephants, 17th-century Indian manuscript illustration

The longest indoor corridor in the world is the *Grande Galerie* in the Louvre, built in 1607 by Henry IV of France. On rainy days the King would clear the entire passageway, move trees, rocks, and grass turf inside, and stage a fox hunt with his entire court down the middle of the corridor.

The Pekingese dog was considered sacred among Chinese royalty. At the court of Li Hsui, one of the last Manchu queens, all court Pekingese had human wet nurses. Each dog had its own eunuch to protect it from other dogs; some even had private palaces, complete with servants.

An elevator was installed in the palace of Versailles in 1743. Run by a series of hand-operated weights, gears, and pulleys, it was used by Louis XV to go from his own apartments to those of his mistress, Madame de Châteauroux, on the floor above him.

An average dinner eaten by King Louis XIV of France: four plates of soup, a whole pheasant, a whole partridge, two slices of ham, a salad, mutton with garlic, pastry, fruit, and hardboiled eggs. At his death it was discovered that the King's stomach was twice the size of a normal stomach.

Cleopatra tested the efficacy of her poisons by giving them to slaves.

In the harem of Mughal kings in India, ladies of royal blood changed their garments several times a day and never put them on again. The once-used costumes were given to slaves.

Queen Elizabeth I of England was completely bald. She lost her hair after suffering smallpox at the age of twenty-nine. To disguise her loss she always wore a wig, thus creating a vogue for wigs in Europe that lasted several hundred years.

Elizabeth I of England owned 3,000 gowns.

The sixteenth-century Indian emperor Akbar often used real dancing girls as chess pieces and an entire garden as a chessboard. Akbar sat high in a marble tower calling each move from his throne and watching the beautiful living pieces whirl from square to square. Two centuries later, in Madras, India, visitors witnessed an equally remarkable sight in the court of the maharajah—chessmen over 25 feet tall, mounted on wheeled platforms and pulled across a giant chessboard by teams of fifty men.

Peter the Great of Russia was almost 7 feet tall.

Safety

There were 24,887,000 automobile accidents in the United States in 1975. In these accidents 46,000 people were killed.

More Americans have died in automobile accidents than have died in all the wars ever fought by the United States.

The death rate for accidents of all kinds is twice as high for males as it is for females in the United States.

Natural gas has no smell. The odor is artificially added so that people will be able to identify leaks and take measures to stop them.

According to the Health Insurance Institute, a person who suffers an accident on a motorcycle has a 90 percent chance of injury or death. A person involved in an automobile crash has only a 10 percent chance of the same. Motorcycles account for 4 percent of all licensed vehicles in America yet are involved in 8 percent of all accidents.

According to the Health Insurance Institute, drivers with the highest mortality rate are those between twenty and twenty-four years old. (Twenty percent of the people killed in automobile crashes in 1975 were between nineteen and twenty-five.) The age group with the lowest mortality rate in car accidents is the seventy-and-over bracket.

The National Safety Council reports that seventy people a day die in home accidents in the United States. Falls account for the greatest number of deaths. Next in frequency are fire, poisoning, electrocution, and choking on food. Most of the people who die from falls are over sixty-five. Middle-aged people and infants die most often in fires. Teen-agers succumb primarily to poison and drugs.

Firemen have the most dangerous job in America.

According to the National Safety Council, ingesting home chemicals such as detergents, solvents, and paint is *not* the major cause of poisoning among children. Children are poisoned most frequently by eating deadly plants.

According to the National Safety Council, a toothpick is the object most often choked on by Americans.

One million people each year are bitten by animals in the United States. Seventy-five percent of these bites are inflicted by wild animals. Approximately 30,000 of the victims must be treated for rabies.

The number of automobile accidents in the United States has been *declining* since 1969.

Motor-vehicle accidents account for 50 percent of all accidental deaths in the United States.

The National Safety Council reports that bicycles, stairs, and doors, in that order, cause more accidents in the home than any other objects.

Two-thirds of all people in the United States who choke to death are under four years of age, according to the National Safety Council.

If a car is moving at 55 miles per hour it will travel 56 feet before the driver can shift his foot from the accelerator to the brake.

Every 45 seconds a house catches fire in the United States.

The Insurance Information Institute reports that there is a motor-vehicle accident in the United States once every eighteen seconds. Deaths in motor-vehicle accidents occur on the average of once every eleven minutes.

According to the National Safety Council, there is one accidental death every five minutes in the United States. There is a major injury every three seconds.

The Sea

When a tidal wave is about to hit a coastline the water first recedes all the way to the horizon. If a person were foolish enough to do so, he could walk out several miles before the wave came smashing ashore.

The Great Wave at Kanagawa, by Hokusai

The Amazon River discharges 4.2 million cubic feet of water per second in the Atlantic Ocean.

The Pacific Ocean encloses an area larger than all the land surfaces of the earth put together.

Ninety-seven percent of the world's water is in the ocean.

If the ice floes of Antarctica were to melt, they would raise the ocean level by 240 feet, submerging a quarter of the world.

Smoking

Tobacco is a food. Though hazardous if smoked, its leaves contain a number of nutritional substances that can sustain life for a time if no other food is available.

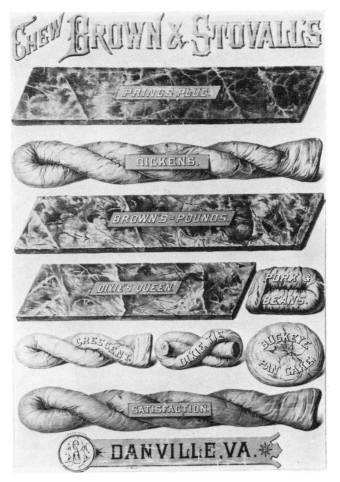

19th-century poster advertising chewing tobacco

In the United States there are 4 pipe smokers, 3 cigar smokers, 3 tobacco chewers, and 1 snuff taker for every 17 cigarette smokers.

Every year, 3 million Americans become cigarette smokers.

Tobacco was originally smoked through the nose. American Indians fashioned a special pipe with a forked end, designed to fit into the nostrils. The smoke was then inhaled through these ends by short, violent snorts. The name of this pipe was a *tubak*—and thus our word "tobacco."

18th-century engraving of pipe-smoking Indian next to tobacco plant

Americans are the heaviest smokers in the world. If the number of cigarettes smoked per day were averaged out individually among the entire population, every man, woman, and child in the United States would smoke an average of two cigarettes a day.

Since 1971, more than 105 new brands of cigarettes have been introduced into the United States.

The average smoker—the smoker who inhales one and a half packs of cigarettes a day—smokes 10,950 cigarettes a year. A heavy smoker may smoke as many as 30,000 cigarettes a year, a nonstop chain smoker as many as 40,000.

A person who smokes one pack of cigarettes a day inhales a half-cup of tar every year.

Sports

Seven thousand years ago, the ancient Egyptians bowled on alleys not unlike our own.

Babe Ruth, one of the greatest hitters in baseball history, began his career as a pitcher.

Volleyball was invented in a Holyoke, Massachusetts, YMCA in 1895. Its inventor was William George Morgan. The game was first called "mintonette" and was played by hitting a basketball over a rope.

Volleyball game in the gymnasium of a New York City school

Abner Doubleday did not invent baseball. Publications about the game were issued as early as 1835, when Doubleday was only sixteen. Further, though he is credited with inventing baseball in Cooperstown, New York, in 1839, it is known that Doubleday was enrolled at West Point from 1838 to 1842. At that time a West Point cadet was not allowed to leave campus until his last years in school; thus it was impossible for Doubleday even to have visited Cooperstown before 1841. Doubleday was, however, distinguished in other ways. He was a Union general during the Civil War and played a leading part in the Battle of Gettysburg.

Runner about to be tagged out in an 1886 baseball game. Contrary to popular belief, Abner Doubleday did not invent baseball.

The Cleveland Indians were named in honor of Louis Sock-olexis, a native Maine Indian who was the first American Indian to play professional baseball. Before it became the Indians, the Cleveland team was known as the Spiders.

An expert fly fisherman may have as many as 10,000 flies in his collection.

Fly-casting tournament, late 19th century

A total of 63 errors were made in the 1886 World Series.

In ancient Greece a boxing match began with two boxers standing face to face, their noses touching. Greek boxers wore leather thongs embedded with metal studs strapped on their wrists. At one time metal spikes were added, too.

In the early days of baseball, between 1840 and 1850, a fielder put a runner out by hitting him with the ball. Home base and the batter's plate were two separate spots (and thus the lineup included a fourth baseman), and there was no distinction between fair and foul balls.

The game of lacrosse was invented by American Indians.

19th-century lacrosse match

Before 1859 baseball umpires sat in a padded rocking chair behind the catcher.

In the 1936 Swaythling Cup Match in table tennis, Alex Ehrlich of Poland and Paneth Farcas of Rumania volleyed for 2 hours and 12 minutes on the opening serve.

The St. Sylvester Road Race in Brazil is witnessed by 1 million people every year.

In the early days of boxing, when a boxer was getting throttled and wished to end the bout, he would take his sponge and toss it in the middle of the ring. Thus originated the phrase "to throw in the sponge."

Detail of *Bare Knuckles,* by George A. Hayes, which depicts boxing in its early days in the U.S.

Survival

A person who is lost in the woods and starving can obtain nourishment by chewing on his shoes. Leather has enough nutritional value to sustain life for a short time.

The average person can live for eleven days without water, assuming a mean temperature of 60° F.

More than 50 percent of the people who are bitten by poisonous snakes in the United States and who go untreated still survive.

According to *Time* magazine (August 6, 1951), the following rule of thumb can be used to determine whether victims of radiation poisoning will live or die:

1. All those who do not vomit after contamination will live.

2. Those who vomit for an extended period of time will probably die.

3. Half of those who stop vomiting within a few hours will probably live.

Theater

Noel Coward wrote *Private Lives* in two weeks.

Toward the end of her life, Sarah Bernhardt had a wooden leg and often wore it on stage. The "Divine Sarah" slept in a coffin, owned her own railroad car, and played Juliet when she was seventy.

James O'Neill, father of the playwright Eugene O'Neill, acted in the play *The Count of Monte Cristo* no less than 5,352 times—an average of one performance a day every day for fourteen years. "I believe," O'Neill once said, "that I should have lost my memory and mind altogether had I continued to keep up the strain."

Slapstick comedy is named after an actual slapping stick. The stick, which came to be equated with broad farce in the sixteenth century as part of the Italian commedia dell'arte, was used by the comic hero Harlequin to whack the rumps of artless stooges. It was made of two pieces of wood joined together to make a slapping sound when it hit.

John Rich, famous English Harlequin of the 18th century, still used slapping stick that originated with 16th-century commedia dell'arte.

John Wilkes Booth was the greatest matinee idol of his era. Though history books rarely mention it, the man who shot Lincoln was beloved and familiar to thousands of theater-goers and was especially popular with women, from whom he received a hundred fan letters a week. In fact, it was Booth's familiarity with the layout of Ford's Theater—he had played there many times—and his friendliness with the stagehands that allowed him to penetrate the security guard so easily the night of the shooting.

Stage bows were originally devised as a way for actors to thank the audience. The audience would or would not acknowledge each of the actors in turn, depending on how much they enjoyed the performances.

Edwin Booth is the only actor in the American Hall of Fame.

Edwin Booth as Iago.
Painting by Thomas Hicks, 1863.

Transportation & Travel

Most automobile trips in the United Sates are under 5 miles.

The first railroad in America had wooden tracks. It was built by Thomas Leiper in 1809 in Crown Creek, Pennsylvania.

To establish how fast a railroad train moves, count the number of clicks heard in twenty seconds. This figure is roughly equal to the number of miles per hour the train is moving.

There is 1 mile of railroad track in Belgium for every 1½ square miles of land.

In 1928 E. Romer of Germany crossed the Atlantic Ocean from Lisbon, Portugal, to the West Indies in a kayak. The trip took him fifty-eight days.

Kayak similar to the one used by E. Romer to travel from Portugal to the West Indies

One method of crossing great expanses of waterless desert used by traders and merchants in the Middle East is as follows: setting out on horseback with their wares, the merchants bring a large number of well-watered camels, which they use as pack animals. At various intervals along

19th-century engraving
of Middle Eastern merchants
loading their camels

the way they stop the caravan and slaughter several of the camels. Then they remove the camel's stomach and give the large amounts of water stored within it to the horses. This water thus sustains their own mounts all the way across the desert and at the same time makes it unnecessary to bring extra stores of water.

The Universe: Stars, Planets, Space

If one were to capture and bottle a comet's 10,000-mile vapor trail, the amount of vapor actually present in the bottle would take up less than 1 cubic inch of space.

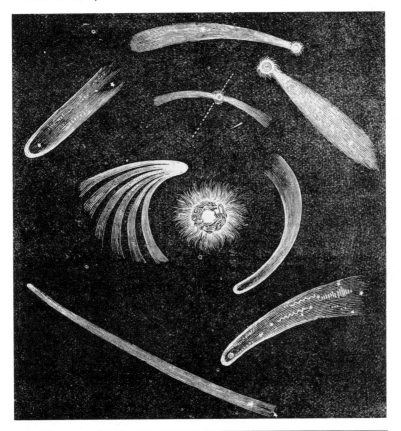

Some of the comets that have appeared over the last four centuries

Members of the Dogon tribe in Mali, Africa, for many centuries worshiped a star known today by astronomers as Sirius B. The Dogon people knew its precise elliptical orbit, knew how long it took to revolve around its parent star, Sirius, and were aware that it was made up of materials not found on earth—all this centuries before modern astronomers had even discovered that Sirius B existed.

Deimos, one of the moons of Mars, rises and sets twice a day.

To an observer standing on Pluto, the sun would appear no brighter than Venus appears in our evening sky.

Saturn's rings are 500,000 miles in circumference but only about a foot thick.

As of 1973 there were more than 5,000 man-made objects flying in space.

It is estimated by scientists that the universe as a whole contains .000000000000000000000000000001 grams of matter per cubic centimeter of space. It is also estimated that the universe is 35 billion light years in size, or 210,000,000,000,000,000,000,000 miles.

Five times as many meteors can be seen after midnight as can be seen before.

The star Zeta Thauri, a supernova, was so bright when it exploded in 1054 that it could be seen during the day.

The star Antares is 60,000 times larger than our sun. If our sun were the size of a softball, the star Antares would be as large as a house.

When we look at the farthest visible star we are looking 4 billion years into the past—the light from that star, traveling at 186,000 miles a second, has taken that many years to reach us.

The telescope on Mount Palomar, California, can see a distance of 7,038,835,200,000,000,000,000 miles.

Hale telescope, Mount Palomar

The sun is 3 million miles closer to the earth during winter than summer.

The diameter of the star Betelgeuse is more than a quarter the size of our entire solar system.

The sun is 330,330 times larger than the earth.

The earth moves in its 585-million-mile orbit around the sun approximately eight times faster than a bullet travels.

It is estimated that within the entire universe there are more than a trillion galaxies (the Milky Way itself contains 100 billion stars). This means that there are probably about 10^{22} stars in the entire cosmos.

Traveling at a speed of 186,000 miles per second, light takes 6 hours to travel from Pluto to the earth.

The sun burns 9 million tons of gas a second. At this rate, it has been estimated, it will burn out in another 10 billion years.

If the sun were the size of a beachball, 21 inches in diameter, and were placed atop the Empire State Building, the nearest group of stars, the Triple Centauri system, would be somewhere in Australia, more than 10,000 miles away. The next "closest" star would be so distant that it would be off the surface of the earth.

When astronauts first shaved in space, their weightless whiskers floated up to the ceiling. A special razor had to be developed which drew the whiskers in like a vacuum cleaner.

A sunbeam setting out through space at the rate of 186,000 miles a second would describe a gigantic circle and return to its origins after about 200 billion years.

The star known as LP 327-186, a so-called white dwarf, is

smaller than the state of Texas yet so dense that if a cubic inch of it were brought to earth it would weigh more than 1.5 million tons.

All the planets in our solar system could be placed inside the planet Jupiter.

Because of the speed at which the sun moves, it is impossible for a solar eclipse to last more than 7 minutes and 58 seconds.

Solar eclipse

Four million tons of hydrogen dust are destroyed on the sun every second.

When the Apollo 12 astronauts landed on the moon, the impact caused the moon's surface to vibrate for fifty-five minutes. The vibrations were picked up by laboratory instruments, leading geologists to theorize that the moon's surface is composed of many fragile layers of rocks.

Apollo 12 astronaut holding container of lunar soil during exploration of the surface of the moon, 1969

If a baseball-sized piece of a supernova star (known to astronomers as a pulsar) were brought to earth, it would weigh more than the Empire State Building.

Phobos, one of the moons of Mars, is so close to its parent planet that it could not be seen by an observer standing at either of Mars's poles. Phobos makes three complete orbits around Mars every day.

A day on the planet Mercury is twice as long as its year. Mercury rotates very slowly but revolves around the sun in slightly less than eighty-eight days.

Statistically, UFO sightings are at their greatest number during those times when Mars is closest to Earth.

According to Professor David Saunders of the Psychology Department of the University of Chicago, abnormally large numbers of UFO sightings occur every sixty-one months, usually at distances from 1,500 to 2,000 miles apart.

U.S. History

During the American revolution, more inhabitants of the American colonies fought for the British than for the Continental Army.

The area sold by France to the United States in the Louisiana Purchase was first offered to England, who refused it. The price paid by the United States for the land, some 100 million acres, averaged out to 4 cents an acre.

The Americans *lost* the Battle of Bunker Hill. They ran out of gunpowder and had to retreat. Further, the Battle of

Battle of Bunker Hill, June 17, 1775

Bunker Hill was not fought at Bunker Hill at all. The actual skirmish took place at Breed's Hill in Charlestown, Massachusetts.

America purchased Alaska from Russia for $7,200,000—about 2 cents an acre.

In the Declaration of Independence as first written by Thomas Jefferson, there was a clause abolishing slavery. Because of popular pressures, however, Jefferson deleted the clause.

Drafting the Declaration of Independence. Thomas Jefferson is 2nd from left.

The Declaration of Independence was *not* signed on July 4th. It was signed in Philadelphia on July 8th, and was first read before Washington's army the following day. Nor did all the delegates sign the document in 1776. Thomas McKean of Delaware did not add his name until 1777. After its ratification, the Declaration of Independence was moved about from place to place, finding shelter in ten different cities and five different states between 1776 and 1951. During this time it twice escaped destruction by fire and was almost captured by the British in both the revolution and the War of 1812. Since 1952 the document has been kept in the National Archives in Washington, D.C.

War & Weapons

Before World War II blacks were not allowed to enlist in the United States Navy.

During World War I the punishment for homosexuality in the French army was execution. If the offender was an officer he was allowed a final charge against the enemy on the understanding that he would get himself shot.

Alexander the Great ordered his entire army to shave their faces and heads. He believed that beards and long hair were too easy for an enemy to grab preparatory to cutting off the head.

Battle of Lexington, April 19, 1775

At the outbreak of World War I the American air force consisted of only fifty men.

One out of every three English males between the ages of seventeen and thirty-five was killed in World War I.

Only eight men were killed in the Battle of Lexington.

Only 16 percent of the able-bodied males in the American colonies participated in the Revolutionary War.

George Custer was the youngest American officer ever to become a general in the United States Army. He made his rank at age twenty-three.

During the Civil War, Robert E. Lee was offered command of the Union Army before he accepted his post with the Confederacy.

In 1221, Genghis Khan killed 1,748,000 people at Nishapur in one hour.

Soldiers in Genghis Khan's army were made into executioners after every battle. The inhabitants of a defeated town were ordered to assemble outside the walls of the town, and each Mongol soldier, armed with a battle axe, was assigned to kill as many as fifty of the captives. As proof that they had carried out their orders, the soldiers were obliged to cut an ear off every victim, collect the ears in sacks, and bring them to their officers to be counted.

Robert E. Lee

The Hessian soldiers hired by the British to fight the colonists during the Revolutionary War were paid about 25 cents a day.

In feudal Japan the Imperial Army had special soldiers whose only duty was to count the number of severed enemy heads after each battle.

During the American revolution soldiers in General John Burgoyne's regiment who misbehaved were not flogged or imprisoned. They were simply made to wear their coats inside-out. Yet so much respect did Burgoyne's men have for their general that his troops had the lowest disobedience record of any soldiers in the war.

The Marine Corps was originally a branch of the British army in the American colonies. The corps was organized in 1740 in New York and was incorporated into the United States military after the revolution.

In Japan there is a deadly martial art, called *tessenjutsu,* based solely on the use of a fan.

Conquering Arab armies in the tenth century used a primitive form of flame thrower and hand grenade. The flame thrower spurted flames of niter and sulphur through copper tubes. Grenades were made of terra cotta shaped to fit the contours of the hand, filled with inflammable naphtha, and covered with relief designs to prevent them from slipping when being thrown.

The Yo-Yo originated as a weapon in the Philippine Islands in the sixteenth century. It weighed 4 pounds and had a 20-foot cord. Louis Marx, the toymaker, introduced it to America in 1929.

Karate, generally considered a Japanese martial art, did not come to Japan until 1916. Prior to this time it was practiced solely by the Okinawa islanders, who had developed it centuries earlier as a means of weaponless defense *against* the Japanese.

The 1905 peace treaty ending the Russo-Japanese War was signed in Portsmouth, New Hampshire. Though the United States had nothing to do with the war, the treaty was arranged and negotiated by United States President Theodore Roosevelt.

Weather

No one has ever discovered two snowflakes with exactly the same crystal pattern.

A thousand tons of meteor dust fall to earth every day.

During the heating months of winter, the relative humidity of the average American home is only 13 percent, nearly twice as dry as the Sahara Desert.

According to Professor Walter Connor of the University of Michigan, men are six times more likely than women to be struck by lightning.

Studies in modern China have found that one can predict

weather with 80 percent accuracy by monitoring the croaking of frogs. A peasant named Chang Chi-tsai devised the following formula, which has been adopted by millions of Chinese farmers and peasants: "If frogs croak on a fine day it will rain in two days. If frogs croak after rain, there will be fine weather. It will continue to rain if frogs do not croak after successive overcast days."

The town of Tidikelt in the Sahara Desert once went ten years without a rainfall.

A bolt of lightning can strike the earth with a force as great as 100 million volts.

18th-century painting showing house being hit by lightning

During a severe windstorm or rainstorm the Empire State Building may sway several feet to either side.

It snows more in the Grand Canyon than it does in Minneapolis, Minnesota.

Lightning puts 10 million tons of nitrogen into the earth each year.

Electrical storm over New York City

In Calama, a town in the Atacama Desert of Chile, it has never rained.

Moist air holds heat better than dry, which is why nights in the desert are cool while nights in the humid tropics are torrid.

The outdoor temperature can be estimated to within several degrees by timing the chirps of a cricket. It is done this way: count the number of chirps in a 15-second period, and add 37 to the total. The result will be very close to the actual Fahrenheit temperature. This formula, however, only works in warm weather.

In 1816 there were frosts and snow in the northeastern United States in every month of the year. Similar weather conditions prevailed in France, Italy, and Spain. The year 1816 became known throughout Europe and the United States as "the year without a summer."

Clouds fly higher during the day than during the night.

We are in the middle of an ice age. Ice ages include both cold and warm periods; at the moment we are experiencing a relatively warm span of time known as an "interglacial period." Geologists believe that the warmest part of this period occurred from 1890 through 1945 and that since 1945 things have slowly begun freezing up again.

At any given time, there are 1,800 thunderstorms in progress over the earth's atmosphere. Lightning strikes the earth 100 times every second.

A rainbow can be seen only in the morning or late afternoon. It is a phenomenon that can occur only when the sun is 40 degrees or less above the horizon.

Salt Lake City, Utah, gets an average of 17 inches more snow annually than Fairbanks, Alaska. Santa Fe, New Mexico, gets an average of 9 inches more snow each year than New Haven, Connecticut.

Weights & Measures

It takes 120 drops of water to fill a teaspoon.

A ten-gallon hat holds less than a gallon.

Tom Mix in a
"ten-gallon" hat

There are two kinds of tons, a regular ton (2,000 pounds) and a long ton (2,240 pounds). There are also two kinds of pounds, an apothecary pound (12 ounces) and a troy pound (16 ounces).

Worms & Sea Creatures

The earthworm *(Lumbricus terrestris):*

can clear and aerate half a pound of soil in a day. (There are, on the average, 3 million worms per acre of fertile soil.)

is hermaphroditic, or bisexual: it can self-fertilize or mate with another of its species.

has several sets of vital organs throughout its body, which is why it can be cut in half and still survive. If it is cut in the middle its two ends will usually regenerate; if it is not cut in the middle one segment will live. However, if it is cut in too many places the whole worm will die.

A hundred tons of barnacles collect on the bottom of a steamship every year.

The snail mates only once in its entire life. When it does mate, however, it may take as long as twelve hours to consummate the act.

Snails under water

When leeches mate, the leech playing the male role (leeches are hermaphrodites and can assume either sex) clings to the body of the female and deposits a sac of sperm on her skin. This sac produces a strong, flesh-deteriorating enzyme that eats a hole through the female's skin and fertilizes the eggs within her body.

Lobsters *do* feel pain when boiled alive. By soaking them in salt water before cooking, however, you can anesthetize them.

At birth barnacles look like waterfleas. In the next stage of their development they have three eyes and twelve legs. In their third stage they have twenty-four legs and no eyes. Barnacles stay fastened to the same object for their entire lives.

When young abalones feed on red seaweed their shells turn red.

Abalone shell

A 4-inch-long abalone can grip a rock with a force of 400 pounds. Two grown men are incapable of prying it up.

The starfish is the only animal capable of turning its somach inside-out. As it approaches its prey (usually a member of the mollusk family), the starfish reverses its viscera, protrudes them through its mouth, and projects them under the shell of its victim. Then it slowly devours the fleshy underparts of the helpless mollusk by a process of absorption.

Sea worms mate in the following way: at mating time, males and females swarm together. Suddenly the females turn on the males and bite their tails off. The tails contain the males' testes and sperm. When they are swallowed and acted upon by the females' digestive juices, they fertilize her eggs.

Snails have teeth. They are arranged in rows along the snail's tongue and are used like a file to saw or slice through the snail's food.

Miscellaneous

The average lead pencil will draw a line 35 miles long or write approximately 50,000 English words. More than 2 billion pencils are manufactured each year in the United States. If these were laid end to end they would circle the world nine times.

The three balls traditionally displayed above pawnshops were inspired by Santa Claus. St. Nicholas, on whom the legend of Santa Claus is based, is said to have turned three brass balls into three bags of gold in order to save the daughters of a poor but honest man from earning their living in dubious ways. Since that time St. Nicholas has been patron saint of pawnbrokers as well as of helpless virgins.

People waiting for pawnshop to open, New York City, 19th century. Three balls on sign were inspired by a miracle attributed to St. Nicholas.

Galileo was the first man to suggest using a pendulum to run a clock.

Turning a clock's hands counterclockwise while setting it is not necessarily harmful. It is only damaging when the time-piece contains a chiming mechanism.

Rubber is one of the ingredients of bubble gum. It is the substance that allows the chewer to blow a bubble.

Of all the world's peoples, the only ones known not to use fire are the Andaman islanders and the Pygmies.

Pygmy hunters in the Congo, one of the two groups of people in the world who do not use fire

Question: When does the twenty-first century officially begin, on January 1, 2000, or on January 1, 2001? *Answer:* Since there never was a year 0 on our calendar, our calendar presumably started in the year 1. Adding two thousand years to the year 1 gives us an official starting date of 2001. However, in the nineteenth century the changeover was celebrated both on January 1, 1900, and January 1, 1901. There is no reason to believe the coming century will not be greeted in a similar way.

Christendom did not begin to date its history from the birth of Christ until 500 years after His death. The system was introduced in 550 by Dionysius Exigus, a monk in Rome.

The average housewife walks 10 miles a day around the house doing her chores. She walks 4 miles and spends 25 hours a year making beds.

Picture Credits

Abbreviations
CP—Culver Pictures
MPG—MPG Picture Collection
NYPL—New York Public Library

7: CP; 8 (top & btm), 9, 10 (top & btm): NYPL; 11: MPG; 12: Museum of Fine Arts, Boston; 13, 14, 15 (top & btm), 16: NYPL; 18 (top): MPG; 18 (btm): Alinari; 19: Museum of Fine Arts, Boston; 22: NYPL; 23 (top): CP; 23 (btm): MPG; 24 (top & btm), 25 (top & ctr): National Library of Medicine, Bethesda, Md.; 25 (btm): NYPL; 26, 28: National Library of Medicine, Bethesda, Md.; 32: Museum of Fine Arts, Boston; 33 (top): The New-York Historical Society; 33 (btm): Alinari; 34: British Museum; 35 (top): CP; 35 (btm): MPG; 36: Museum of Fine Arts, Boston; 39: A.T.&T. Co.; 40: CP; 41: The Metropolitan Museum of Art, N.Y.; 45, 47: NYPL; 48: CP; 50 (top & btm): MPG; 53: Miami Seaquarium; 54; 55 (top & btm): NYPL; 56: **The Oxford Book of Food Plants**, by B. E. Nicholson, Oxford University Press; 57, 58 (top): CP; 58 (btm): Hunt Botanical Library, Pittsburgh, Pa.; 59: The Metropolitan Museum of Art, N.Y.; 60: NYPL; 61: CP; 63 (top): NYPL; 63 (btm): CP; 64: NYPL; 65: National Gallery of Art, Washington, D.C.; 66: CP; 67: The Metropolitan Museum of Art, N.Y.; 69: CP; 72 (top & btm), 73: NYPL; 75, 77: CP; 79: NYPL; 81: Muzeul de Arta, Craiova, Rumania; 83 (top): MPG; 83 (btm): Museum of Fine Arts, Boston; 84: MPG; 86: NYPL; 89 (top & btm): MPG; 90: **Treasure Island**, by Robert Louis Stevenson, Harper & Bros., 1921; 91: MPG; 92: CP; 98: Society of Antiquaries, London; 99: NYPL; 101: **Book of Pirates**, by Howard Pyle, Harper, 1903; 102: CP; 103: NYPL; 104: Library of Congress; 107: CP; 108: Private Collection; 109: NYPL; 110, 111 (top): CP; 111 (ctr): The Metropolitan Museum of Art, N.Y., Crosby Brown Collection; 111 (btm): MPG; 114, 115 (top & btm), 117: NYPL; 118: MPG; 119: NYPL; 120: MPG; 122: Library of Congress; 123: NYPL; 124, 125: MPG; 127, 128: CP; 129: MPG; 132: NYPL; 133 (left): Library of Congress; 133 (rt), 134, 135: MPG; 136: CP; 137: MPG; 138: Library of Congress; 140, 141: MPG; 143: CP; 146: MPG; 147: Library of Congress; 148: The Metropolitan Museum of Art, N.Y.; 149: NYPL; 150: MPG; 152: NYPL; 154: The Metropolitan Museum of Art, N.Y.; 155: Tobacco & Textile Museum, Danville, Va.; 156, 157 (top & btm), 158: NYPL; 159: MPG; 160: NYPL; 161: MPG; 162: National Gallery of Art, Washington, D.C.; 164, 165: MPG; 166: National Portrait Gallery, Smithsonian Institution, Washington, D.C.; 167: NYPL; 168, 169: MPG; 170: CP; 171: Hale Observatories; 173: NYPL; 174: National Aeronautics & Space Administration; 175, 176: NYPL; 177: Insurance Company of North America, Philadelphia, Pa.; 178, 179: MPG; 181: The Library Company of Philadelphia; 182: CP; 184, 185, 186 (top & btm), 187: NYPL; 188: CP; 189: Paul Travis, The Cleveland Museum of Natural History.